In the Long Run We Are All Dead

A MACROECONOMICS MURDER MYSTERY

Second Edition

Murray Wolfson
California State University–Fullerton

and

Vincent Buranelli

St. Martin's Press
New York

Senior Editor: Don Reisman
Project Editor: Joyce Hinnefeld
Text Design: Cohen & Steins
Cover Design and Art: Tom McKeveny

For information, write:
St. Martin's Press, Inc.
175 Fifth Avenue
New York, NY 10010

ISBN: 0-312-01881-9

But this *long run* is a misleading guide to current affairs. *In the long run* we are all dead. Economists set themselves too easy, too useless a task if in tempestuous seasons they can only tell us that when the storm is long past the ocean is flat again.

——John Maynard Keynes
A Tract on Monetary Reform (1923)

About the Authors

Murray Wolfson is Professor of Economics at California State University–Fullerton. The author of scholarly works on international conflict resolution and Marxian economics as well as a principles text, Professor Wolfson (Ph.D., University of Wisconsin, 1964) has also taught at several universities abroad and been a Fulbright Lecturer in Japan.

Vincent Buranelli is a professional writer. The holder of a doctorate in history from Cambridge University (England), he has written numerous biographies and other works and has coauthored an encyclopedia of espionage.

Preface

If *In the Long Run We Are All Dead* is to live as a macroeconomic murder mystery, it must change with the times. Even so, readers of the first edition will find their old friends still hard at work learning economics to find "whodunnit." In the midst of economic crisis, presidential adviser Admiral Harcourt Green is murdered while trying to decide between competing economic policies. Navy Lieutenant Alice Ritter's understanding of the competing sides' underlying ideas leads her through a twisted path toward solving the murder.

But the problems and theories of the first edition, those characterizing the first Reagan administration, are different today. The macroeconomic issues are not immediately double-digit inflation and interest rates. They are the "twin deficits" in the federal budget and foreign trade that threaten to destabilize the new order. The Wall Street meltdown and the gyrations of the dollar show how much we have traded the rigid aspects of macroeconomic central planning for the hazard of instability in a market-determined economy.

Yet the macroeconomic ideologies that Alice must decipher still divide along the same fault line. Keynesians advocate governmental intervention for short-term stability and social welfare. Those who search for the long-run efficiency of an unregulated, competitive economy regard market breakdown as a transient part of the overall adjustment process. But because no program has proved able to solve all our problems, partisans of each side are sharply divided, even among themselves.

For the planners, our Chairman of the Council of Economic Advisers, Murray Sokolow, is still the traditional Keynesian. He believes that macroeconomic policy can engineer the economy if he can negotiate a social contract between competing interests. But his neo-Keynesian protégé, Howard Tilson, now even less sanguine than before about the stability of the system, insists that the management of demand be directed to favor the less privileged.

Monetarists are no longer the sole advocates of the rule of market forces. Federal Reserve Chairman Christopherson now has his critics within the Board of Governors. His critics claim that monetarism makes too many concessions to Keynesian concepts. These new classical economists advocate efficient markets based on rational expectations. A new personage appears as the protagonist for the supply-side economists. Geraldine Anderson argues sharply for low taxes and growth, expressing a view which has risen from voodoo status to orthodoxy among lip-reading policy makers.

We hope our book remains good clean fun. We have tried to be evenhanded in expounding the quarrels of contentious economists. Along the way, we have shown a bit of the politics of policy making. In this effort, we wish to express our gratitude for the help—and amused tolerance—of students, fellow teachers, and generally supportive reviewers. We should particularly like to thank Ellen Mutari of The American University and Allen Blitstein of Southwest State University, who read an early draft of this edition in its entirety and offered helpful advice. They saved us from some awkwardness and mistakes, but are not to be held responsible for the final product. We plead guilty to our errors and throw ourselves on the mercy of the reader.

Murray Wolfson and Vincent Buranelli

Contents

1

Prologue to Mystery

Lieutenant Alice Ritter glanced at the clock on her desk. Almost time to leave the White House, she thought as she rummaged in her shoulder bag for her cosmetics case. Admiral Green never liked to be kept waiting. And, she knew as well as anyone, today's meeting with the President and the cabinet was of crucial importance. The President's chief of staff had to be on time.

Taking a mirror from the case, Lieutenant Ritter held it up before her face and gazed at her reflection. She saw black eyebrows neatly penciled, high cheekbones, a snub nose, a mouth slightly upturned at the corners as if about to break into a quizzical smile, a firm chin, and smooth, lustrous, darker-than-tan skin.

"Black *is* beautiful," she told herself with satisfaction untinged with false modesty. "Even in the navy."

The telephone broke into her thoughts. Pushing the case back into her bag, she raised the phone and cupped the receiver to her ear. "Admiral Green's office," she said. "Lieutenant Ritter speaking."

"Alice," came the reply, "this is Green. I'm at the Pentagon library. I've finished my report. Pick me up, will you?"

"Yes, sir. I'll be there soonest. It won't take me long, not on Sunday. No traffic to buck."

"Good enough. I'll be waiting for you."

Minutes later Alice Ritter eased the naval staff car out of the White House parking area onto Pennsylvania Avenue. She made the turn at the corner of Fifteenth Street and headed south past the Treasury and Commerce buildings. She made a

1

loop to the left by way of Constitution Avenue that took her along Fourteenth Street. Now she crossed the Mall with the Washington Monument to her right.

The tall shaft gleaming in the bright sunlight was an inspiring sight, but Alice had no time to pause for a second look. She increased her speed, flanked the Potomac Tidal Basin, passed the Jefferson Memorial with its familiar colonnades, and reached the George Mason Bridge over the Potomac River. Once across, she filtered into the approaches to the Pentagon.

The center of the United States' military might appeared, from the outside, rather foreboding. The edifice stood huge, ugly, and comparatively silent. On any other day of the week, cars would fill the extensive parking lots. Crowds would be streaming in and out of the building—movers and shakers of world power. Generals and admirals who had made or lost reputations in Vietnam would be there, along with foreign dignitaries from places as different as Afghanistan and Israel.

Those three places—Vietnam, Afghanistan, and Israel—were often mentioned by military leaders who argued that the United States should avoid long wars of attrition, avoid traps like Vietnam. The Soviet defeat in Afghanistan told the same story of superpower failure in a protracted struggle against guerrillas maneuvering on their own terrain. Israel's Six-Day War offered a better example of how to wage war today. Before you get into one, be sure you can win it with one lightning thrust.

These thoughts were in Alice's mind as she slipped into a parking spot. She got out and walked over to the guard at the entrance. He made a brief call.

Hanging up, he said, "Admiral Green wants you to wait. He hasn't finished his report yet."

Alice returned to the car, got in, and pulled the door closed. She waited patiently, expecting to see Admiral Green at any moment. The minutes ticked away, until nearly an hour had gone by.

"It's taking the admiral a long time," she reflected. "I

thought he said he had finished his report. Oh well, that's economics for you!"

Alice gazed idly at a group of men who emerged and stood talking near the entrance. A woman came into view behind them, a tall, good-looking brunette, spangled in jewelry, carrying a briefcase. Passing the men with a purposeful stride, the woman entered the parking lot. She passed so close that Alice could see a petulant expression on her face. She got into a car and roared off.

A few minutes later, Admiral Green appeared. Tossing his briefcase into the back seat, he climbed in beside Alice. He was wearing a business suit, as he usually did since becoming the President's chief of staff. But he still looked every inch the career naval officer he had been when he commanded an aircraft carrier task force on maneuvers in the Mediterranean. Now fiftyish, he had cold gray eyes, iron-gray hair, and the rolling gait of a sailor.

"Let's go, Alice," he said. "Back to the White House."

"You're still early for the cabinet meeting, sir."

"Good, let's go by way of the Lincoln Memorial."

Alice turned on the ignition, backed out of the parking slot, and headed into the clover-leaf pattern north of the Jefferson Davis Highway. Green was silent, ruminative.

Alice broke the silence. "By the way, I saw Geraldine Anderson while I was waiting for you."

Green looked interested. "Geraldine Anderson," he repeated the name. "The latest guru of supply-side economics. The new kid on the block over at the Commerce Department. I wonder what brought her to the Pentagon on a Sunday morning."

"Well, sir, she looked mad about something."

Green laughed shortly. "Every economist I know is mad about something. They all think they have the right line about our economic problems, and they don't like being contradicted. It's me and my friends against all the others. And we're right.

"I know where Geraldine Anderson stands," he went on. "Heard her sound off at a party Frances threw at our place. Jerry would be right at home in the administration. Since I know her supply-side formulas, I don't have to ask her opinion about our current crisis.

"Just as well," Green reflected. "She's one sarcastic lady. I'd just as soon not talk to her one-on-one."

Silence fell again for a few minutes. "By the way," Green said, "how do you happen to know Geraldine Anderson? She hasn't been in Washington more than a few weeks. I didn't know she existed until Frances introduced us."

"I don't really know her," Alice explained. "I just heard her give a talk on economics and politics a week or so ago at the American University here in D.C."

Presently they were rolling across the bridge. The Watergate Hotel complex and the Kennedy Center for the Performing Arts, off to the left, became visible on the opposite shore. The Lincoln Memorial lay straight ahead.

"Admiral, you visit the Lincoln Memorial a lot, don't you?" Alice commented.

"Yes. I find it consoling, especially when I've got a tough decision to make. Lincoln knew how to make tough decisions. That's one reason he was able to save the Union."

"The Confederacy might have won the Civil War in the short run," Alice observed. "The North might not have survived those disasters when the fighting began."

"Which just goes to show," Green pointed out, "that it's not always wise to plan for a long war. You might be defeated by an enemy who moves quickly against you. That was the secret of the German blitzkrieg in World War II. They won their campaigns in the west before their enemies could do any real fighting. But when their blitzkrieg failed and they got bogged down in a long war in Russia, they lost. Lincoln, on the other hand, was able to adapt to changing circumstances. He survived the early defeats, planned for a war he knew would be a long one, and won it.

"The long run and the short run! How often success lies in knowing which to choose. And how seldom is the choice an easy one."

The car reached the shrine to the martyred President at the

edge of West Potomac Park. Alice curved left along the circular drive, past a number of movable barriers painted with red and white diagonals, and reached the front of the memorial. A police officer, recognizing the naval staff car, waved the admiral and the lieutenant on into the restricted parking area.

They mounted the front steps and stood in front of the monumental statue of the President who saved the Union. Lincoln seemed to be rising from the chair to greet them. They gazed without speaking at the somber, furrowed face and the deep-set eyes. They were scarcely aware of the chatter of Sunday visitors around them.

Admiral Green ended his brief meditation. "Okay, Alice. Let's get to the White House. I'm ready to report to the President."

Continuing to the left on the circular drive, they entered Bacon Drive. This took them on a diagonal to the corner of Constitution Avenue. Alice slowed down as a green light turned amber and then stopped as amber gave way to red. Ahead of them stood the National Academy of Sciences, unmistakable because of the statue of Einstein in front. They looked directly at a large, spreading juniper bush on the academy grounds. Not a soul was in sight.

While the motor idled, Alice leaned down from the steering wheel and tugged at the heel of her left shoe.

"You know, Alice," the admiral said, "an economic crisis is tough because half the time you can't tell who your real enemy is. Inflation, unemployment, or————"

Green broke off in mid-sentence as if he had been suddenly throttled. His head jerked back violently. Then he collapsed heavily against Alice, jarring her so hard that the wheel twisted to one side. Frantically she struggled to control the vehicle despite the weight forcing her against the door. It took her but a split second to realize what had happened. There was a hole in the windshield on the right side. Glancing sidewise, she saw another hole between the admiral's eyes. Blood was flowing from the back of his head, a crimson stain spreading over the shoulder of her uniform.

Only a bullet could do that kind of damage. A sniper had shot Admiral Green. The shot had come, must have come, from the juniper bush just ahead of the car. Almost by reflex, Alice Ritter slammed the accelerator to the floor, desperate to escape before the sniper could fire a second shot.

The car zoomed forward in a burst of speed through the red light and along Constitution Avenue past the Federal Reserve Building. Alice careened up Seventeenth Street, trying to hold down the hysteria rising within her. All she could think of was that she must get to the White House before she broke down. Driving to the hospital was out of the question. The sniper had hit Admiral Green with a single, well-placed shot. He was dead.

Alice's mind was beginning to fog over when she jolted to a stop at the White House gate. She heard as if at a great distance a babble of excited voices and shouted commands. Then she was being helped out of the staff car and into the Executive Mansion. A bottle of smelling salts waved under her nose brought her reeling senses into focus, and she found herself surrounded by men she knew, members of the White House Secret Service.

She heard a man say, "Lieutenant Ritter, are you well enough to tell us what happened?"

Alice took a deep breath to steady her nerves. "Yes, I am," she gasped.

2
Warning Signs

As her words tumbled out, Alice Ritter had at the back of her mind the thought that the wheel had come full circle. It had all started right here in the White House on the previous Thursday.

That was when President Wedik presided over an urgent meeting on the nation's economy. Admiral Harcourt Green was there as the President's chief of staff. Wedik relied on Green to direct traffic during the discussion, to keep the arguments in focus, and to decide what to do after hearing from two economists who came to the conference with opposing formulas. One economist was Murray Sokolow, an Ivy League professor whom Wedik had enticed out of retirement to head the Council of Economic Advisers. The other was Martin Christopherson, former banker, now chairman of the Board of Governors of the Federal Reserve System.

These four men assembled in solemn conclave because the United States stood on the brink of an economic catastrophe that threatened to make the Great Depression of the thirties pale by comparison.

Before the meeting came to order, Wedik looked at Green as if to say that the President was totally dependent on the admiral to guide him through this economic maze.

But Green himself was having a problem. The economics he learned at Annapolis was not enough to give him any guidance in a national crisis. He knew the basics, and that was about it.

He brought Alice Ritter to this conference because she knew more about macroeconomics than he did—she had taken two years of it in college before gaining admission to the U.S. Naval Academy.

Just now, Alice was doing some heavy thinking. When Christopherson mentioned inflation as they were settling into their chairs, she recalled the time when Green persuaded her father to join him in a real estate venture in Dallas.

Chief John Ritter, an old navy buddy of Green's, wanted to invest the money he had managed to accumulate. But he was worried about inflation.

"Never mind that," Green had said. "We'll gain by inflation because we'll pay off our mortgage on the buildings in cheap dollars. While the interest seems high, after the gain we make from inflation, the real rate of interest will actually be low."

John Ritter was not so sure. Wedik's predecessor, the late President John Allen Curtin, had been elected on an anti-inflation platform. Ritter said to Green, "What if the President does stop inflation? How are we going to pay off our mortgage if our income from rents goes down along with other prices?"

Green had a persuasive answer. "That would be okay too. In the long run, when inflation doesn't have to be factored into interest rates, the rates will come down. We'll borrow at the new low interest rates. We can pay off the old high-interest loans, and make payments at the lower figure. We'll refinance our debt."

"The long run." Ritter lingered thoughtfully over the words. "I just hope it won't be too long. We'd be really speculating, wouldn't we?"

"Sure," Green agreed. "But speculation isn't a dirty word. Why not go for the megabucks out there? Navy pay won't make either of us rich."

Alice remembered vividly the scene when her father signed the agreement. She was still not entirely sure he had done the right thing.

Then there was that other scene, when Admiral Green gave the commencement address when she graduated from Annapolis. She heard the admiral saying things that surprised her.

"Don't concentrate on money," he exhorted the graduating men and women. "Lift your heads above the money-grubbers out there in the world you are about to enter. Remember that you are naval officers. Duty comes first."

As Admiral Green droned on, Alice could not help thinking about the very different words he had used when he was urging her father to join him in the Dallas real estate venture. "Which is the real Admiral Green?" she wondered as she sat in the corps of newly minted naval officers listening to him.

When Alice became Admiral Green's aide, she put her doubts behind her. Green knew about her because of his friendship with her father. He had helped get her the appointment to Annapolis. She had ambitions for sea duty—even a command. But for now she was working shore duty with high-level responsibilities at Green's side.

Green shifted in his chair. Christopherson's reference to inflation made him think of the Dallas venture and of how his views had changed since the apartment-house agreement was signed. He was no longer as sure as he had been when persuading Chief Ritter to join him. Of course, many economists had reasoned as he had done. But under President Curtin's anti-inflation program, the economy had declined disastrously.

Green began to think that the economy was suffering calamitous withdrawal symptoms from inflation. The warning signs seemed clear to him in hindsight. Contracts, debts, expectations, mortgages, speculation—all had been built on the belief that inflation would continue. People were protecting themselves from inflation by taking on debts they could pay off in cheap dollars. They felt this was a better course than saving their money, which would depreciate in value as prices rose. These people were caught in a catastrophic money squeeze as monetary restriction made loans carry record-high interest rates.

When prices stopped rising and started to nose down, those who were in debt could not meet their fixed payment obligations. Farms and businesses went broke. Paralysis spread to other segments of the economy.

The speed and magnitude of the depression made it look like 1929 and 1932 all over again. President Curtin had collapsed under the strain. The heart attack that carried him off was a release.

Vice President Wedik took over with bold promises to lick the country's financial problems.

The new President said he would continue to fight inflation as the long-term enemy by persuading the Federal Reserve Board to stabilize the growth of the money supply. He would reduce interference by Washington in the national economy. He would balance the budget.

Green understood that this line was the advice Wedik was getting from Christopherson and his monetarist advisers.

At the same time, Wedik was getting advice from supply-side economists. He said that, above all, he would cut taxes. That would leave more money in the hands of people who were productive. It would stimulate investment in new equipment and thereby accelerate economic growth. In this way the economy would right itself.

How sound were the arguments? Could Wedik cut taxes and fight inflation at the same time? Wouldn't he end up with a huge federal budget deficit? Green would have to make up his mind on that before he could advise the President about how to handle the present crisis.

Wedik was not a man to act resolutely on his own. Petrified by the whipsaw of events, he could not rise to the occasion. The country sensed his indecision, and the consequences were disastrous.

Green found it hard to forgive Wedik his inability to make up his mind. Right or wrong, a command decision had to be made, and the nation had to be reassured. Franklin Roosevelt had managed to convince a terrified American people in 1933 that "the only thing we have to fear is fear itself." But Wedik was paralyzed by fear, and it was contagious.

And now everything came down to this meeting in the Oval Office. It was Thursday, and the President was trying to decide what to do by Sunday, when answers to hard questions would have to be provided at a cabinet meeting and broadcast to the American people.

3

Crisis in the Oval Office

"Okay, let's see what we can come up with," Wedik said. "Admiral Green, do you want to say something?"

Green nodded. "We're in a crisis situation," he addressed Sokolow and Christopherson, "and the first thing the President needs from you is a clear description of what's happening. Let's get that straight, and then we can look at our options."

Christopherson spoke quickly. "We've got to make it clear that we do not intend to go off half-cocked. We won't rush government into the breach every time there's a temporary problem. We have to let the markets come to equilibrium through supply and demand."

Sokolow parried the thrust that was obviously aimed at him. "Well, what do you expect the government to do? Should we sit on our hands while the economy goes to hell in a handbasket?"

Christopherson's voice rose. "That's not what I mean, and you know it. During the stock market meltdown of 1987, the Fed acted to stabilize the market by stimulating the supply of credit."

Sokolow became personal. "Yes, and you caught hell from your 'perfect market' friends! They think nothing should be done to direct the economy. The market will take care of everything by itself. Ridiculous!"

Christopherson flushed. "Some of my colleagues at the Fed thought we didn't go far enough, and some thought we went too far. I don't deny it. They've been pushing me pretty hard. The supply-side people want me to ease up on the money supply, to let the markets provide greater growth. And the 'new classical'

11

people are saying that no systematic stabilization policy enacted by the Fed can really influence events."

Green broke into the argument. "What are you saying about the plan we need?"

"Well, I'm a monetarist," Christopherson said. "No matter how we differ at the Fed, we all agree that the market will provide full employment in the long run. Short-term employment does follow the money supply, but only at the cost of reducing *real* wages because money wages lag behind inflation. There is no permanent growth in employment to be gained by inflationary increases in the money supply. What is needed is steady growth in money to match production potential without attempting to force the situation. The Fed will not abdicate control of the money supply, but we will not constantly intervene in a market that will take care of itself best if left alone."

"So?" Green drew him out.

"We've got to make it clear that we will not be pressured into allowing the quantity of money in this country to change drastically in the present crisis. We must pledge that the money supply will grow no more than economic growth. We can't expect foreigners to stay calm while we threaten to increase or decrease the money supply with every change in the rate of interest or every rise in the unemployment figures."

Sokolow had been listening with impatience. Now he broke into Christopherson's monologue. "I deny that money is at the heart of our crisis! Let's see why the demand for goods and services has dropped so dramatically and do something about it, instead of worrying about what foreign speculators might do. Let's get our workers back on the job. Let's get business back to investing in machinery and equipment. To do that, we are going to have to drive down those ruinous interest rates."

Christopherson started to say something, but Sokolow kept talking volubly and loudly. "You monetarists insisted on a fixed money supply regardless of the changing demand for money. That made interest rates go violently up and down. No wonder businesspeople can't buy capital equipment, or consumers carry any installment purchases! When the rates are so high, nobody can afford to borrow for investment! You've given us 1932 all over again! The recent volatility of interest rates is having a devastating effect on investments, the stock market, and the value of the dollar! Your inflexibility is indefensible!"

Stung by the accusation, the normally decorous Christopherson faced his accuser. "You're blaming the only responsible element in or out of government for the present mess! Starting from Keynes's *General Theory* in 1936, the Keynesians thought they could make the economy work by flooding it with paper money. Instead of having the courage to let supply and demand get the country out of the Depression, they found flunkies to increase the money supply. What did the country get for it?"

Wedik wondered what he would answer if called upon, but of course the rhetorical question was directed at Sokolow.

"I'll tell you what," Christopherson went on. "We got a commitment to produce too much money to chase too few goods. We got inflation. Inflation is the cause of the high interest rates."

Admiral Green interrupted. "Christopherson, why do you say that interest rates are high because there is too *much* money?"

"Because interest rates have to be higher than the expected rate of inflation, and due to financial irresponsibility, the expected rate of inflation is now out of control."

"And you, Sokolow, say that the interest rates are high because there is too *little* money?"

"Yes, Admiral, because interest is the price that people have to pay for liquid cash from banks and other lenders. The restriction of the money supply to meet mindless, arbitrary goals set by the monetarists is what keeps interest rates high. It's simply a matter of supply and demand for money."

The Oval Office fell silent for a moment. A bird twittered outside the window. Rays of sunlight slanted through the panes onto the floor. Green digested what he had just heard. He broke the silence by stating the terrifying truth. "Then President Wedik must make a command decision on the basis of contradictory advice."

The two economists looked at the President, who stared back at them without uttering a word. Desperately he turned to his chief of staff.

Admiral Harcourt Green knew what he had to do. He rose abruptly and put himself between the President and the others. "Thank you very much," he said to Christopherson and Sokolow. "I'll get in touch with you later. I need a lot more facts. Lieutenant Ritter will set up the appointments. In the meantime, we all will consider this conversation as security classified."

When the two economists were gone, Green poured Wedik a double scotch. The admiral had enough experience to know that neither courage nor judgment came out of a bottle, but Wedik clearly was not able to exercise either of these characteristics of command. Alcohol was the most appropriate sedative at the moment.

"Mr. President, I'll go to my office for a moment and arrange for appointments with those two."

Wedik nodded dumbly. Green went to his White House office, where he found Alice Ritter at the typewriter.

"Alice, the President and I need a chance to talk quietly together. He has been under a tremendous strain." Having seen one breakdown, Lieutenant Ritter did not have to guess what Green feared. "I want you to cancel the President's meetings for the rest of the weekend. Get the chief on the phone, and arrange for a trip on the *Chesapeake* down the river."

Even to Alice, Harry Green often referred to John Ritter as "the chief." While Harry Green had worked his way up to admiral's flag rank, John Ritter had paralleled Green's advance in the enlisted ranks. Ritter had achieved the rank of chief warrant officer, which lay in limbo between the enlisted who rose through the ranks and those who were commissioned. Now, after retirement, Chief Ritter was the civilian captain of the *Chesapeake*.

Ritter and Green had been more than comrades in arms. There was the lifelong mutual respect between the experienced naval officer and the chief who made the navy work. John

Ritter's ultimate promotion to chief boatswain spoke as much for his character as Harry Green's achievement of flag rank had spoken for his.

"After you do that, Alice," Green continued, "set me up afternoon appointments with those two economist prima donnas, Christopherson and Sokolow. I'll call on them at their offices. Like it or not, it looks as if I'm elected damage-control officer on this economic ship, and the first step toward staying afloat is a condition report."

By the time Admiral Green rejoined Wedik, the President was ready for his third scotch. He had regained some of his composure at the cost of losing some of his inhibitions. He needed a friend, a confidant.

"I'm glad we finished with those economists, Harry. They were getting on my nerves. I can't tell what they're fighting about."

"Neither can I, Mr. President. Some of it is the same sort of infighting that people do out of jealousy over careers and status. There certainly is enough of that in Washington. But more is involved. They are opposed to each other on economic principle."

"Maybe it's because they are so close on so many things that they can't stand the disagreement. It looks like a family quarrel to me."

"I'm sure you're right," Green said. "The curious thing is the quarrels within quarrels. Christopherson as a monetarist is dead set against Sokolow for being a die-hard Keynesian. But it seems there are some even more thoroughgoing free-market advocates in the Fed. I'm told they consider Christopherson a dinosaur because he won't increase the money supply fast enough."

Wedik looked miffed. "You must mean the supply-side appointees," he said defensively. "That was Curtin's idea. He put them there to make American industry more competitive. He said if they didn't push the Fed to stop holding back on the money that could be loaned to the government, we would have to raise taxes to cover our budget."

The President chopped both hands in the air in an emphatic gesture. "For Curtin, new taxes were *out*. He said they just sapped initiative and reduced output. In the end, they would bring in less money to the government. People can't pay taxes unless they're earning income, can they?"

Green beat a retreat. "I'm sure you're right, sir," he said again. This time his tone was deferential. "I agree with your basic game plan to let the market solve the problems involved in our economic dilemma."

Wedik was mollified. "You know, Admiral, I'm not a dogmatic person."

"Yes, sir, I know."

"I followed Curtin's lead. I did what he told me he was going to do. I kept Christopherson in office as a monetarist. I appointed supply-side people. I also appointed people who call themselves 'rational expectations economists' to important positions."

"Yes, sir, different people as Curtin said. But you also put your own people into important positions. That way, you could compare ideas and make up your own mind as Chief Executive."

"That's right. I wanted people with sound thinking. Not just college professors. Businesspeople who have met a payroll. Sound union leaders who know how to negotiate a workable contract."

"Mr. President, you were wise to call Sokolow back into the chairmanship of the Council of Economic Advisers. He gave you another perspective. You knew he was something of a zealot coming from a Keynesian position."

Wedik shrugged. "I heard that from Christopherson. But I had no choice. I was the second man on the team, and the second man gets stuck with all the failures of the boss."

Wedik was back to a subject he understood. The liquor had loosened his tongue. He was oblivious to the fact that Green had heard it all before.

"The only reason I was put on the ballot as Vice President was to balance the ticket. There was no way the party was going to win the election unless it had somebody from the Midwest with a labor base. That would balance John Curtin and his Orange County, California, mafia. We didn't have much in common, but he knew he needed me."

"Well, I'm sure you were needed, Mr. President," Green hastened to agree.

"Yes, I was needed because without me the labor people never would have voted for John Curtin. Plenty of plumbers and carpenters had high taxes and inflation up to their ears, but they were also mighty strong union members. They voted for us because inflation was eating into the gains their unions got for them faster than they could renegotiate their contracts. They figured the government was taking money away from them by inflation and taxes, and giving it away to people on welfare. They thought their jobs and seniority were being taken away by government affirmative action programs. They didn't like the government giving our money away to foreigners in foreign aid programs. All that aid didn't do labor any good—all it did was raise taxes. At least that's the way it looked to the ordinary white working man in Chicago and Gary, Indiana."

Wedik was being carried along by his own remembered campaign oratory but Green redirected him. "Yes sir, but what would make them wary of John Curtin? Isn't that what he was complaining of in his campaign, too? It seemed to me that you were in perfect agreement."

Slightly befogged, Wedik stared at the admiral. "Well, of course we were in agreement, Harry, but you have to understand that we were different. The blue-collar workers knew they could trust me. They didn't feel that way about John Curtin."

"So you are saying, Mr. President, that labor wanted its interests protected under a new administration, and they feared that Curtin would represent the business interests against theirs."

"Sure. So there was an agreement and a difference. It came out in a lot of ways. Take a tax cut, for instance. Curtin wanted to cut taxes to increase savings and give people incentives to work. Well, whose taxes should be cut? The rich or the skilled-labor middle class?"

"Yes, I see."

"And then, as you recall from the primary election campaign and the flare-up at the nominating convention, these differences got hardened into questions of who would get political appointments, and what states would get government projects, and so on. You've seen enough of politics to know how that goes."

"Sort of like our two economists. Whatever they may have started arguing about in universities and government offices, it's also become a hassle over who gets promoted, who gets a salary increase, and who gets to build an empire of assistants.

"All organizations work that way. Wasn't it that way in the navy?"

Green smiled. "Yes sir, it was. I guess I could tell you some stories, too."

Wedik swallowed a mouthful of liquor and went on. "Well, like in any organization, the solution to gaining power was a coalition. In this case, Curtin rode the crest of the anti-big-government wave, and I was nominated as Vice President to bring along the rest of the vote. My record as Senator from Illinois was what Curtin needed to put us over the top."

Wedik was on familiar ground. He had been an extraordinarily successful figure in the Congress. All the skills at negotiation that he had acquired in his years as president of the electricians' union, and then on the executive board of the Building Trades Council of the national labor organization, stood him in good stead in the Senate.

Curtin and Wedik had swept the election. And now Harcourt Green was asking Wedik what had gone wrong. He was encouraging the President to keep talking.

Wedik was only too ready to do so. "When Curtin took office, he and Martin Christopherson began a program of restricting growth in the money supply. We had included that as part of our campaign program to fight inflation. I really don't understand how the money supply is created or destroyed. You will have to find out about that for yourself."

"Yes sir, I will."

"Christopherson was always talking about the long run. Politically, that's nonsense! Our administration didn't have ten years to bring down the rate of inflation. We were voted in to do something about inflation right now."

"Yes sir, I remember. All of us were in trouble."

"So the new administration had to produce results, and sooner than you might think. Congressional elections are only two years after the presidential election. Take away the time spent switching administrations, making new appointments, getting the show on the road. That costs you almost half a year before you shake down. Then figure that your policies have to be seen to be working for maybe six months before the congressional election day to do any good in getting voters to support your candidates."

Green nodded. "That leaves not much more than a year to show results. And if you don't show results and then lose control of the Congress, you never will carry out your program."

"You got it, Harry. And you won't get reelected at the next presidential election. Suddenly you're a one-term President. A loser."

"So President Curtin pressed the Federal Reserve to cut the money supply more aggressively. Then what?"

"Well, then there was hell to pay, that's what." Wedik refilled his glass. "We caught it from one group after another. People were yelling that they couldn't borrow money from banks and savings and loans to buy houses. The savings and loans were yelling that they couldn't get anybody to deposit money with them, so they had nothing to lend. The lumber industry was pounding on the White House door because they couldn't sell to the housing industry. I caught pure hell from my old friends in the building trades union. Even fellows who had worked with me years ago wrote to complain that I had sold them out."

"More than the housing industry was affected," Green suggested to give Wedik another subject.

"Sure, everybody was in favor of fighting inflation as long as it was the other guy who had to get along with less money. That's what killed Curtin. He was dead politically even before he had his stroke."

The ice in Wedik's drink tinkled against the glass. He used two hands to set it down. "Then it was up to me. I had to restore public confidence and national unity.

"That's when I called Sokolow. I don't know if he is right or Christopherson is right. I admit it, Harry. Maybe they are both crazy. But I had to bring Sokolow in. He was the guy who talked about planning for full employment. That book he wrote about the full-employment economy being the efficient economy caught on. Do you remember—they even had it on television. If we were all working full blast, he said, then the 'size of the pie' to be divided up would be bigger. We wouldn't have capital and labor fighting. We could do something for the blacks without taking jobs away from the whites. He really had it all figured out."

"But he was out of favor after a while."

"Yes, for a while. That was when he got blamed for inflation. We didn't make him the fall guy in our election campaign because he was so popular. We pinned inflation on the other party. But there is no doubt that he didn't seem to be Superman anymore. Still, when unemployment started up again, he was running the only game in town."

"And now he and Christopherson are at it."

"You heard them. We have until Sunday night to decide which way to go. I'm the fall guy this time. What happened to John Curtin scares the hell out of me. What should I do?" Wedik made another attempt at his glass. Tinkle, spill, and all, he got it to his mouth.

Harcourt Green made his move to strengthen Wedik's nerve and encourage him to think of himself as an able Chief Executive. "Mr. President, I think you have done an outstanding job in holding the country together. I can see how skillfully you have been able to manage the crisis thus far. And I must say I am proud to serve under you."

20

Wedik leaned back in his chair and accepted the light Green offered to the President's cigarette. After Wedik's puff of smoke, Green went on, "I think that in any war, victory goes to those who do good staff work as well as to those with able commanders. This administration needs some staff work and quickly. Let me start from scratch and find out what really is going on in the economy out there. I'll make some sense out of this four-way rhubarb: Keynsians, monetarists, supply-siders, and new classical economists. As soon as I get it sorted out, I'll get back to you."

A second puff.

"In the meantime, Mr. President, sir, why don't you take a break on the *Chesapeake?* I will do the spadework and you can have a chance to think the situation over away from all the details. You can be back by Sunday for the cabinet meeting. Chief Ritter may be retired, but he runs a good ship. You need perspective, sir."

A pause. "Okay. That sounds like a good idea."

"I'll have Alice Ritter arrange for you to slip out to the *Chesapeake* without a lot of media coverage."

"Okay."

Admiral Green had taken command.

4

A Domestic Quarrel

President Wedik disappeared into the private living quarters of the White House. Admiral Green returned to his office.

"All set, Admiral," reported Alice Ritter. "You're to meet Sokolow at the Old Executive Office Building at two. And Christopherson at the Fed at four."

"Good enough, Alice. Well, it's eleven o'clock. You might as well knock off till the first conference. I need a break before I face those two fanatics. Meet me at the Old Executive Office Building. I may need your college Economics 101 expertise."

Green sat for some minutes in the empty office, until the phone called him away from his musing. It was his wife.

"Harry," she said, "I want you to come home for lunch."

"What for? I've got things to do at the White House."

"You'd better come," Frances Green insisted. "Professor Howard Tilson is here. He's an economist I met at the Beautify America conference.

"I know about your conference!" Green was exasperated.

"Well, I didn't mean to upset you," Frances answered soothingly. "The point is that Professor Tilson phoned this morning and wanted to know if there was any chance of meeting you, the President's right-hand man. It struck me that lunch today would be a good occasion, if you could make it. You're not tied up as far as I know. Are you?"

"No, not really. I can get away for an hour or so."

"Well, please do. Professor Tilson asked if he could bring a friend along. A supply-side economist. Naturally I said yes. So, they're both here. They don't agree on anything. Professor Tilson was a student of Murray Sokolow, you know. It might be good for you to hear what they have to say. And I know they'll be flattered to meet you."

Green considered the proposal. He knew his sessions with Sokolow and Christopherson would be grueling. A talk with two other experts might not be a bad idea, especially in the privacy of his home. "I'll be there," he told his wife.

But before leaving his office, he dialed a number in Georgetown.

"Marianne van Thuys," said a dulcet voice with a touch of a Continental accent.

"Marianne, can we meet tonight? I want to talk to you."

"Of course, darling. We'll drink that Armagnac you brought back from Europe. When will you be at the apartment?"

"Around six. My last conference today is at four."

Green heard a familiar chuckle. "What about your wife?"

"Frances can wait, as she always does. And as always, she won't know why."

"You don't think she suspects about me?"

"How could she? We've been discreet. And not just because of Frances. The last thing the President needs is to have the *Washington Post* come out with a headline about the sex life of his chief of staff."

Marianne considered the point. "What about your aide?" she inquired at last. "That black girl who thinks she's a sailor?"

Green was offended. "Alice Ritter *is* a sailor, Marianne. I wouldn't be surprised if she holds a naval command some day." Then, feeling that his tone was too blunt for the occasion, he continued in a conciliatory manner, "Anyway, whatever Alice knows or thinks she knows, she's an officer who would never weaken the command authority. She won't talk. And certainly not to Frances."

"I'm glad to hear it, Harry. A woman in my position can't afford a scandal either. Well, darling, I'll expect you around six. We'll talk about—things we've talked about before."

Green drove to his house, a large one on the outskirts of Washington. As he came in sight of the building, he was startled to see that a party was in full swing. A number of guests were walking around the grounds. A chatter of voices drifted through the open windows.

"A party at noon!" Green thought explosively. "Frances wanted me to come home so I can play the performing bear for her beautiful people! It's the last time she does this to me!"

Resisting a temptation to turn around and return to the White House, he drove between red brick gates and along a gravel path that curved gently past a sculpted lawn and well-trimmed landscape shrubbery. He stepped onto the portico and saw the rooms filled with guests grouped around the various punch bowls and buffets. He thought of the many times Frances had insisted on dragging him into soirées with her high-toned friends she knew he could not abide.

She usually had the latest abstract artist to put on display for her own amusement and her husband's irritation. What was it about a canvas daubed in garish colors and stuck with miscellaneous bits of junk that seemed to fascinate Frances? Collages of wire, twine, and bits of paper; piles of bottles and tin cans; riveted metal plates that looked as if they came from a used car lot—they had no meaning for Green.

Still, the admiral felt there was something Frances understood about these things that was beyond him. Her accomplishments might even have been a point of pride with him except that he could not escape from the avant-garde esthetes who invaded his home and preoccupied his wife. No protest or complaint would change her. She had acquired her esthetic taste and her liberal sympathies at college, and they were now second nature to her.

Frances had brown hair and striking light blue eyes. She had kept her good looks. She gave her husband a peck on the cheek, pushed a martini into his hand, and led him over to where three of her guests, two men and a woman, were surrounded by a dozen-or-so others. She pushed through the group, dragging him by the elbow.

The woman had her back to them. She turned around as Mrs. Green called out, "Jerry!"

The admiral found himself facing a tall, dark-haired woman with a regal bearing, shrewd expression, and level gaze. He started as if embarrassed by this sudden encounter with a beautiful, forceful member of the opposite sex. His hand shook, spilling half the martini onto his jacket. He covered his confusion by pulling a handkerchief from his breast pocket and dabbing at the stain.

"Well really, Harcourt!" Frances exclaimed. "I hope Jerry doesn't have that effect on every man who crosses her path. Well, meet Geraldine Anderson. Jerry's frightfully smart. Knows all about supply-side economics."

Green flushed, pushed the handkerchief back into his pocket, and extended his hand.

Geraldine Anderson gave him a firm handshake. She looked him straight in the eye. "I'm pleased to meet you, Admiral," she said. "But don't take your wife's introduction too seriously. Grew up on a farm in Ioway. I'm better at potting rabbits with a .22 than at solving the country's economic problems. I haven't been in Washington long. Just got a job at the Commerce Department."

Green fumbled for words. "I'm sure they appreciate you over at Commerce," he said.

He seemed relieved when Frances steered him toward the others. "This is Professor Howard Tilson," she said. "You know Captain Greg Algernon."

Tilson was a young man whose overly large beard contrasted strangely with his slight build. Algernon was a ruddy-faced naval officer in uniform.

Algernon picked up on something he had been saying. "Tilson, you claim the government should spend money to make work for the unemployed. But where is the money coming from?"

Tilson took a sip from his cocktail. "Nothing simpler, Captain. There are three ways for a government to raise money—taxation, borrowing, and creating new money. This means———"

"You mean printing it?" Green interjected bluntly.

"Well, it's done by the Federal Reserve extending new bank credit, but it amounts to the same————"

"Easier money alone is not enough," Geraldine Anderson interrupted before Green could follow up his question. "It has to be accompanied by lower taxes for investors."

"Printing money causes inflation," Algernon put in, pleased he could make a point.

"Well, we need both money creation and borrowing," Tilson went on. "The new money will help the government fight unemployment. Reduced taxes on lower-income groups will encourage consumer demand to fight depression. I think————"

Anderson refused to let him get the words out. She seemed to be baiting the professor. "Low taxes for investors are beneficial even in a booming economy. They will bring in more and better high-tech equipment. Everybody will produce more because they have greater incentives. That's supply-side economics, and I'm all for it!"

Tilson shook his head. "Supply-side economics! Trickle down!" he scoffed. "Jerry, it's just a giveaway to the rich. We need tax relief for consumers—workers, the middle class.

Anderson shot back, "Lower taxes on business increase output and prevent both inflation and economic slowdown. Let's protect the *supply* side, and everybody will benefit."

"Well, I say we should ease the money supply and lower taxes to stimulate *demand,*" Tilson retorted. "That's the right way to get increased output."

There were titters among those listening. Somebody said, "Trickle down or trickle up. You two seem to be approaching the same thing—increased output through easy money and lower taxes—from opposite directions. Liberal or conservative, the French have an expression for it: *Les extrêmes se touchent*—opposites meet. Right?"

Tilson grinned. "Touching sounds good, Jerry. Let's give it a try," he said suggestively. "That might be fun."

Her voice developed a hard edge. "Don't push your luck, Howard. It might run out on you."

26

Now the two economists were fencing. Tilson was excited by his beautiful opponent. Anderson, on the contrary, was a study in self-control. She looked directly at her host.

"Admiral Green, will you come to a lady's defense?"

Green coughed behind his fist. "I don't think you need any help from me, Ms. Anderson," he said lamely.

"Admiral, you're too gallant," Tilson intervened. "Supply-side economics is not a great alternative theory like classical supply-and-demand economics, Keynesianism, and monetarism. Supply-siders claim to be descended from classical economists, but they're its illegitimate offspring."

Anderson confronted Tilson as if no personal remarks had passed between them. She was obviously bent on scoring debating points. "I am a supply-and-demand market-oriented economist," she said. "It's just that I believe those monetarists who won't increase the money supply sufficiently are obsolete. They're fighting antiquated battles with the Keynesians and are starting to sound like them. The Fed should increase the money supply enough to make credit easier. That will prevent high interest rates from negating the good supply-side results of tax cuts."

"You have just given us the formula for the present crisis," Tilson stated. "Supply-side tax cuts plus all that military spending created the inflation. Moreover————"

Anderson spoke sharply. "No! The supply-side program didn't fail. The markets here and around the world didn't have the guts to give it time to succeed. Economic growth will eliminate inflation."

"You're just avoiding hard choices."

"Such hard choices wouldn't have to be made if supply-side policies were in place."

Anderson glanced at Green, who was staring into his martini glass. Frances Green had been listening intently, shifting her gaze from one to the other. Now she lofted a question for anyone who could catch it to answer. "Why shouldn't the government lower taxes and just borrow when it needs money?"

"There's the deficit," Algernon said, looking as if he had made a profound observation.

"The deficit will come down," Anderson replied, "as lower taxes increase output and enlarge the tax base. We should reduce government spending to cut taxes."

Tilson had a ready answer. "Deficit financing makes sense during periods of unemployment, as Keynes said. But at full employment, supply-side thinking is voodoo economics because output can't be rapidly increased. Then tax cuts are simply inflationary."

Anderson tilted her head in a sarcastic gesture. "Increased output means more goods and less inflation. After all, inflation is too much money chasing too few goods. So we need more goods. Simple."

Green was prompted to ask the big question on his mind, "What can we do in the present crisis if inflation heats up?"

"Cut military spending, for one thing," Tilson said.

"Out of the question," Green replied bluntly. "Weakening our defenses would be an invitation to the Soviets to take dangerous gambles, maybe even war if they thought they could win quickly. We can't rely on arms-control agreements alone."

"Let's spend the Russians into the ground! They can't match us," Algernon exclaimed.

"Arms or welfare, guns or butter," Tilson balanced the terms. "I vote for welfare and butter."

"That's short-sighted!" Anderson snapped. "We should stop pouring money down a rat hole. Cut taxes in the higher brackets. Then the lower brackets will gain as a result of better jobs. Forget Keynes."

The onlookers were beginning to lose interest in all this economic theory. They drifted away, and the party started to break up. One by one the guests offered their thanks to their host and hostess and departed.

Geraldine Anderson was the last to go. "I'm sure we'll meet again soon, Admiral," she said. "After all, we're both interested in economics. We have a lot to talk about during this national emergency."

Green nodded, making no reply. A moment later he and his wife were left alone in an otherwise empty house.

The admiral was irritated. "Frances, why do you have to have a shindig before lunch? It's bad enough at night."

"Some of my friends can't make it at night. They're performing at the disco."

"I don't like some of your friends!"

His wife gave him a hard look. She spoke with calculated animosity. "I don't like some of your friends. One of them, anyway."

Her words gave Green an uneasy feeling. "What do you mean by that?"

"You know what I mean. You know what you've been up to." Frances was working herself up into a rage. "There's no use trying to brazen it out. I know why you get home late so often."

"I've been working late at the White House."

"Sometimes. And sometimes you've been 'working late' at an apartment in Georgetown!"

The savage undertone in her voice revealed a side of Frances Green unknown to her friends. Even the admiral rarely saw it, but when he did, he realized that under that silky exterior there was a tough, strong-minded, strong-willed woman whom it might be dangerous to cross.

Her husband, too, was becoming angry. "Say what you mean!" he demanded.

Frances obviously enjoyed her next thrust. "I've had you watched!"

"You what?" Green nearly choked on his fury.

"Oh, don't be so self-righteous! I only did what I had to do. A few weeks ago, when you said you were working late at the White House, a friend of mine saw you in Georgetown. Another time I phoned your White House office and Alice Ritter told me you had gone home a couple of hours before. Only you weren't home. So where were you? I decided to find out.

"That's why I hired a private detective. He's been following you. He brought me his report this morning. I know where the apartment is. I even know her name—Marianne van Thuys!"

They stood glaring at one another when the shrill ring of the phone made them both jump. Frances, closest to it, picked it up. Getting a grip on herself with an effort, she spoke pleasantly into the instrument.

"Frances, this is Alice Ritter," she heard. "I'm checking with Admiral Green about this afternoon."

The two women exchanged a few pleasantries, and then Frances handed the phone to her husband.

"It's one-thirty, Admiral," Alice said. "You've got that appointment with Sokolow at two."

"Thanks for the reminder, Alice. I'm on my way. Meet me there."

He put the phone back in its cradle and looked thoughtfully at his wife.

"Frances, we haven't been getting along for a long time," he said. "You know that. We used to satisfy one another's needs. That's not true anymore. It's not just that I don't like your friends—you humiliate me in front of them. Look what just happened here. You tricked me into coming home, and you made me feel like a fool. No one could blame me for wanting to get away."

"I blame you! It was your coldness that made me like this. I had to rely on my friends. Now I know you've been seeing another woman. And you have the nerve to get mad because I found out!"

Green looked uncomfortable. "Well, we've got a problem, and I don't see any way out. We can't trust each other anymore. I suppose you think I put Alice up to phoning so I could have an excuse to leave now."

"After what I've learned, I'd believe anything of you!"

Green became sarcastic. "You don't mind if I go to the Old

Executive Office Building, do you? You won't have me shadowed by your private eye?"

"Not if you stay away from Marianne van Thuys!"

"Maybe you'd like to chaperone me and see for yourself that my appointments this afternoon are on the up and up? Two o'clock at the Executive Building; four at the Fed."

"I'll stay here," Frances snapped, "and decide what to do. I've just about had it with you!"

Green stared at her reflectively for a moment. Abruptly he turned his back and left the house. His wife heard the car door slam and the motor roar. The sound circled the driveway and died out down the street.

5
Dilemmas of the Marketplace

Alice Ritter walked briskly to the Old Executive Office Building. The headquarters of the Council of Economic Advisers was a gray stone baroque wedding cake, each floor of its facade embellished with columns and the ornamentation of a bygone era. She mounted the broad stone steps, halted for a security check, and was allowed past after an assurance from Sokolow's office that she was expected.

Alice arrived there just before Admiral Green came in. Sokolow himself greeted them and led them through a high-ceilinged reception area. Its turn-of-the-century ornate white walls gave it a somewhat academic appearance despite the battery of secretaries at work.

Even though he had but recently moved in, Sokolow's office in the back showed the mark of its occupant. The desk was cluttered with books and papers. More books lay in piles along the walls, and some were scattered on the sofa. Sokolow had to pick up an armful to find places for the admiral and his aide.

Never before apologetic about the disarray in which he worked, Sokolow now felt a twinge of remorse. His mind flashed back to his days in the Marine Corps. He knew that Admiral Green would be thinking "gear adrift" as he looked around the office. And Sokolow did not want to do anything to alienate the admiral.

To the chairman of the Council of Economic Advisers, the issue was stark. The safety, perhaps the very existence, of the

United States depended on his effectiveness in persuading this proxy President of the correct economic policy for this time of extreme crisis.

The admiral spoke first. "Mr. Sokolow, I'm here to listen to your point of view, and then I'm going to talk to Christopherson at the Federal Reserve to hear him out as well."

"When will you see him, Admiral?" Sokolow asked.

"When I leave here. After I see him, I'll think about what I've heard and draw up a report."

"Since you're on a tight schedule, Admiral," Sokolow said, "I won't mince words. In my opinion, Christopherson with his monetarism is basically the same as the supply-siders and the so-called 'new classical' people who have joined him at the Fed. All of them have a blind faith that full employment, control of inflation, and international balance will all come about by the working of the marketplace without the government lifting a finger."

Sokolow was satirical. "If prices are too high, there's an excess of supply and prices fall. If prices are too low, there's a shortage and prices rise. The market is supposed to find the right price at which there is neither shortage nor surplus. That's what they mean by clearing the market."

"I suppose you don't believe the law of supply and demand can clear the market for each and every good and service offered for sale?" Green asked.

"No, although that law was once unquestioned. That's why John Maynard Keynes's book *The General Theory of Employment, Interest and Money* caused such an uproar in 1936. The book impressed economists at the time because it explained mass unemployment. Before Keynes drew the right conclusions from the unemployment, the old-guard theory of supply and demand said the market should function automatically."

"And so," Green observed, "unemployment would be eliminated at some market-clearing wage, since labor is bought and sold like canned goods or dresses or any other commodity."

Sokolow nodded. "But the classical school—pre-Keynesians like Alfred Marshall—turned out to be wrong about supply and demand. This 'new classical' school—Christopherson mentioned it at the White House this morning. They talk about 'rational expectations,' but they still maintain the infallibility of supply and demand. They say individuals acting on what they know, however imperfect their knowledge, project what they think will happen into the future, and move the market toward stability. This too is a false theory because it's based on a blind faith in market equilibrium."

Sokolow leaned forward to press his point. "Unemployment lasted from the 1929 crash of the stock market until our involvement in World War II in 1941. Keynes saw the same thing in England, and he realized something was wrong with the classical theory because it could not explain mass unemployment for extended periods of time."

Green shrugged. "Economists before Keynes couldn't help discovering unemployment."

Sokolow twisted in his seat. "Of course, but they believed unemployment was temporary and self-correcting. If workers were willing to take the equilibrium wage at which the market cleared, then it was only a matter of time before unemployment forced them to change their minds."

"So unemployment was considered voluntary in the sense that people would rather be unemployed than take lower pay."

"Exactly. But whatever sense voluntary unemployment might have made for short periods of time, or for particular industries, it simply did not square with the facts of universal long-term unemployment. The issue is, what is the *cause* of involuntary unemployment?"

"What I don't understand is how there could *not* be enough demand for the goods produced," Green said. "After all, the value of goods must somehow end up equal to the money received by people to make those goods. How can they *not* have the money to make up the demand for everything produced?"

"What you're describing is Say's Law."

"Who was Say?"

"I can tell you that," Alice volunteered. "Jean Baptiste Say was a French economist of the early nineteenth century. 'Supply creates its own demand' was his watchword."

Sokolow nodded at her like a professor complimenting a student. "The trouble with Say's Law was that it treated the economy as if it were a barter economy instead of a money economy. The value of the produce *is* equal to the payments to those who produce it: rent to land, wages to labor, interest to capital, and profits to entrepreneurship. But there is no reason to believe that people will spend their money. They can hold on to cash and not buy anything. They can put it in the bank. Business might not borrow those savings to invest in new equipment."

"So, if people spend their money," Alice interjected, "then something like Say's Law makes sense."

Sokolow added the negative side of the argument. "If they won't spend, you have to ask under what circumstances they will. The trick is to control how much people spend."

"Can't that be done by controlling the amount of money they have?" Green questioned. "It's easy to create new money through the Federal Reserve."

"Sometimes, Admiral. But Keynes taught us that there is no simple relationship between the quantity of money and spending. To the extent that there is a cause and effect relationship, it involves interest rates. Increasing the quantity of money drives interest rates down toward their minimum value. At lower interest rates, firms as well as individuals are able to borrow and spend."

Green pursed his lips. "Sokolow, you're telling me that an increase in the money supply makes people spend more. I don't see what you're quarreling about with the monetarists. They say the same thing."

Sokolow frowned. "Well, that's what the new classical people say against the old-fashioned monetarists. But we feel that interest rates, once at the minimum, could not be driven down any further by increasing the money supply."

"That's the liquidity trap, isn't it?" Alice suggested.

"Yes, Lieutenant."

"Are we in this liquidity trap now?" Green asked.

"No, Admiral, but it could happen. Interest rates can't go to zero, after all. Besides that, interest-rate reduction won't stimulate investment very much if business prospects are already poor and firms have excess capacity."

"So all in all, Say's Law holds only if people spend all the money they earn," Alice continued.

"Right," Sokolow agreed. "Without adequate spending there would be unemployment. Some products would be unsalable. Employers would lay off workers. Those workers couldn't buy consumer goods, and there would be more layoffs. Inadequate demand would make the Gross National Product fall."

"I see," Alice said. "We have to find out why people spend their money for consumption and investment."

"Right again. Demand for the GNP is demand for consumption and investment, as well as foreign demand for our exports, and our government's demand for goods and services."

Green intervened. "What would you have the Council of Economic Advisers recommend in case private spending was not enough to maintain demand for GNP at a full-employment level?"

Sokolow looked at him. "Monetary or fiscal policy. Monetary policy would increase the money supply to drive interest rates down. That would make it more attractive for businessmen to borrow to invest in new capital equipment."

"Would that do the trick?" Green asked.

"Not always. Interest rates might already be at their minimum."

"Why would it fail?" Green wondered. "The liquidity trap?"

Sokolow knew that nobody had found evidence of an absolute minimum interest rate, and that Keynes himself was not dogmatic about liquidity traps.

"Well, there might not be an actual trap in the full sense," he confessed, "although it seemed there was one in the 1930s. Business was too pessimistic to invest no matter what the interest rate. Today, we might be afraid of inflation again if we had to pump enough money into the economy to overcome the caution of battered business executives. So many dollars might drive the value of the dollar down on world markets. Other countries might take that to be a price war in cheap dollars to grab export markets, and they could retaliate. So the world money supply could zoom out of control!"

Green pressed on. "What if monetary policy didn't work?"

"Fiscal policy," Sokolow stressed. "The government's power to spend and tax. When unemployment is high, spend more and tax less. Government spending can take up the slack in the private sector."

Sokolow sounded so positive that Green and Alice fell silent while they considered this line of thought. Alice tugged at a strand of her hair. Green tapped his fingertips together.

Alice spoke first. "What would the monetarists do?"

"They would mouth some claptrap about allowing the market to work." Sokolow said. "They might even mention the possibility that under unemployment conditions, prices would eventually fall, and the money that people spend would be enough to restore employment."

"That sounds reasonable to me," Green told him.

"It might be so in the long run, after the people had endured prolonged unemployment and business bankruptcies. But I'm not interested in the long run. In the long run we are all dead, Keynes used to say."

"But aren't the long-run implications important?" Alice asked.

Sokolow glared. "Lieutenant, we have mass unemployment. The rest of the world is ready to dump the dollars they own. We've got a ship ready to founder if we don't man the pumps and steer back to port. And you're lecturing me about possible long-term implications."

Before he could say more, the telephone shrilled. Sokolow picked it up. He listened briefly to the voice on the other end.

"Of course, Mr. President," he replied. "I'll be right over."

Hanging up, Sokolow told his two visitors, "The President wants me to go to the White House and review a letter on trade policies he's sending to the Japanese premier. But of course he's giving our present discussion highest priority. So I won't be gone long. Just a trip to the Oval Office and back. Meanwhile, make yourselves comfortable—and think over what I've been saying. We'll pick up on it when I return."

He put his briefcase under his arm, went out into the corridor, and headed for the exit.

6

Mixed Motives

Alice stretched and got to her feet. "Sir, I think I'll take a tour around the grounds if you don't need me. I can use a break after all that economics."

"Go ahead," Green replied. "I'll stay here and do some thinking about what we just heard."

Alice left, and Green began to ruminate over the economic problems confronting him. If only there weren't so many, and if only they weren't so complex! If only————"

A voice from the doorway broke into his thoughts. Green turned his head and saw Howard Tilson.

"Mind if I drop in?" Tilson asked. "I saw Dr. Sokolow leave the building, and when I spotted you in his office, I figured you'd be alone for a while."

Green explained that Sokolow had been summoned to the White House. "What are you doing here?" he inquired of the bearded economist.

"Checking some facts and figures in the files of the Council of Economic Advisers." Tilson sat down in the chair Alice Ritter had vacated. "I want to tell you how much I enjoyed your party."

"Well, you helped keep the party going with all that talk about Keynes."

"Don't hold the master responsible for everything I said," Tilson commented. "Today there are all kinds of variations on his themes. Sokolow and I have had some merry go-rounds on the question of where Keynes stands now. He thinks more like an engineer of economic solutions than I do. Still, all us Keynesians regroup when we go into battle against the free-market types. They also do a lot of infighting. Jerry Anderson is caustic about Christopherson restraining the money supply. By the way, what did you think of Jerry?"

Green hesitated. "Eloquent on supply-side economics," he ventured.

"Eloquent," Tilson repeated the word. "Not persuasive, though. The supply-siders are dead wrong, as I pointed out to her. Anyway, Jerry is more interesting than her economic theories. She's dazzling, wouldn't you agree?"

"Oh, I agree," Green said. "But don't you think we should discuss economics? That's what I'm here for."

"Sure," Tilson responded, and immediately returned to the subject he really wanted to talk about. "Jerry's a puzzle. She could have had a top position in the California banking system. Prestige, power, big bucks, the works. Turned it down to take a second-rate place in the Commerce Department. Told me so herself when I first met her over there. Said she just wants to be in Washington. But from the way she said it, I'm sure that's a secondary motive. I'm betting her real motive is some man. I think she came to Washington because he's here."

"Well, that's her business," Green said curtly. "I don't think we should be discussing it."

Tilson chuckled. "I understand your reticence, Admiral."

"You do?"

"Yes, you have a personal interest in Jerry."

"Ridiculous! I just met her!"

"I know that. She asked me to introduce you to her. The President's right-hand man conferring with the economist from Iowa, and all that. But as an officer and a gentleman, you don't think it's proper to pry into a lady's personal affairs."

"That's right."

"However, I'm a bachelor," Tilson went on, "and I wouldn't mind squiring Jerry around Washington. I haven't got to first base so far. I can't help wondering who my rival is. Probably some hack in the Commerce Department."

"No doubt you are correct," Green stated. "That's the place

40

to look if you have to. But why not drop it? There are plenty of available women in Washington."

Tilson grinned. "I can vouch for that. But how many will cause an admiral to spill his drink at first meeting?"

Green scowled. "A pure accident. It's not the first cocktail I ever spilled. You can quote my wife on that."

Realizing he had made a slip, Tilson stopped grinning. "I'm just kidding, Admiral." Realizing also that Green did not want to continue the conversation, he added quickly, "I'd better get out of the way before Sokolow returns. I've got some inflation data to study. Admiral, call me any time you want the pure milk of the word on Keynesian economics."

"I will," Green assured him.

Tilson slapped his hands on his knees, rose, waved a hand, and departed. Green tried to pull his thoughts together after the interruption.

Alice returned. "I'm ready for the second act with Dr. Sokolow," she commented.

"So am I, Alice."

7

Banking and Battleships

When Sokolow reentered his office, he tossed his briefcase onto a pile of books and sat down behind his desk. "Well then, where were we? Oh yes, I was about to say something about inflation and unemployment." The professor was back in action, lecturing his class.

"I'm listening," Green said.

"Between the price level and unemployment there is a complex interaction of aggregate supply and demand. The aggregate supply curve shows that when the GNP and employment rise, so does the price level."

"Inflation?" Green prompted him.

"Yes, especially under conditions approaching full employment. There the classical theory makes more sense than during a depression. Wages are bid up, labor unions become more powerful, supply bottlenecks appear, and prices rise accordingly. If union wage demands are so high as to be unrealistic even in a strong market, some workers are priced out of the market, and we have both inflation and unemployment."

Green nodded. "But if workers are unemployed in a generally tight labor market, it must be that they can't get those skills that are in demand. Maybe they can't adapt. Maybe they are discriminated against on the basis of race, sex, or age."

"Sure, that is what we call structural unemployment. The structural rigidities cause firms to raise prices rather than hire new workers to increase output."

Sokolow pushed at the stack of books on his desk. "As a matter of fact, a tight labor market tends to solve these problems, although it's a long-term process during which there may be too much inflation."

"All right then, why doesn't all this work in reverse?" Green argued. "Why not let wages and prices fall during a depression? Then unemployment will cure itself."

Sokolow nodded his understanding of Green's point but added, "Wages are sticky downward in a depression, but not upward in inflationary periods."

"Isn't that what is called 'money illusion'?" Alice asked.

Sokolow flinched. The word "illusion" had drawn fire from those academic economists who believed it was always possible to explain human behavior rationally.

"It's an unfortunate phrase," he admitted. "But it does point out that workers sometimes focus on money wages rather than real wages."

"Are you arguing," Green inquired, "that money wages are what they are because the workers are under an illusion?"

"Well, Keynes did seem to suggest such an idea in the depths of the Great Depression, but we really are discussing the relatively slow decline in wages during periods of unemployment rather than some illusion."

Admiral Green frowned and fingered his tie pin. He was tired of all these economic abstractions and historical illusions. He wanted something practical. "What do we do now that we have both rising prices and unemployment?"

"We'll have to make a trade-off to meet employment objectives. Perhaps price and wage controls to limit inflation."

"Isn't that bureaucratic and inefficient?" Green protested.

"I don't think we'll have to go as far as controls. Merely to threaten to adopt them can get a reasonable limit on inflation, at least for the short run."

"And what will you do in the long run when people see you're bluffing?"

"Face that if it comes," Sokolow declared bluntly. "Nothing is worse than mass unemployment. I think it makes no sense to talk about being efficient when our labor force can't find jobs."

"So at this point you'd use monetary and fiscal policy to increase demand?"

"Right. I would have President Wedik go after Christopherson at the Federal Reserve to get interest rates down. Despite the so-called independence of the Fed, the President has lots of leverage and usually gets his way. He can get them to reduce interest rates. The Fed has a variety of means."

"Such as?" Green asked.

"Such as going into the open market to buy back government bonds and Treasury Bills. The Fed will write checks on its own unlimited credit to pay for them. That will pump money into the system as banks collect from the Fed. It will lower interest rates and increase investment. And it will raise prices on the stock and bond markets."

"Do you think monetary policy alone will stop this unemployment situation even though it failed in 1932?"

"I think we should try it. But I don't think that will be enough."

Sokolow was on his feet pacing. "The situation is so grave now that fiscal expansion is the only way. Government must bridge the gap between private spending and the amount of money needed for full employment."

Green appeared unimpressed. "I suppose you mean make-work projects like the WPA during the Depression of the thirties. Or giveaway programs."

"Frankly, Admiral, I'd like to see more money spent on those activities. The WPA did a lot of good things—like building libraries, parks, and dams—that private enterprise wouldn't do. Anyway, it doesn't make much difference from a macroeconomic point of view what the money is spent on. Even battleships will do."

Sokolow bit his lip and sat down, but the admiral took the slip in good humor. "Well, as much as I would like to have new battleships, it seems absurd to say it makes no difference how we spend our money. I'm bothered by the thought of government spending more at this time. Surely we should be saving our money and putting it to work. I'm not a wealthy man, but what I do have is the result of saving my money, not spending it. That way, I was able to buy my real estate holdings. The rest of my savings stayed in the bank."

"And the bank stands ready to lend those funds to business," Alice supplemented his observation.

"Well," Sokolow said, "I think it's a mistake to generalize one's own experience to the economy as a whole."

"The whole is not always the sum of its parts," Green suggested.

"Exactly." Sokolow was back on his feet. He controlled the didactic wagging finger with an effort. "I'm reminded of the paradox of thrift. Keynes showed that if people decided to save more than they had previously, the result might be less saving than before."

"Well, if they save a larger portion of their income, I can't imagine how they end up saving less. This is some hocus-pocus dreamed up by an odd academic."

"No sir, that is not so!" Sokolow's voice rose. "The point is that a decision by individuals to save more means they will spend less. The GNP will decline. There will be less income to save from, and hence savings will fall. Besides, people save smaller portions of their incomes when their incomes are down. So you have a smaller income to start with, and a smaller portion of it saved."

"But," Alice commented, "you do agree with Admiral Green in explaining how an individual accumulates wealth by saving?"

"Yes, of course. Taken one at a time, we all increase our wealth by saving, and, of course, by investing. But the same is not true of the nation because the demand for investment arises from different motivations than those influencing the supply of savings. Investment depends on profit opportunity as seen by businesspeople. And savings depend on the aggregate national income or GNP."

Green frowned. "Let me try to understand you, Dr. Sokolow. You're saying first and foremost that the problem of unemployment comes from inadequate demand."

"Right, Admiral."

"You don't believe the market forces of supply and demand

will automatically set prices and wages at a level where demand meets supply at full employment levels of output."

"Right again. I do not believe in Say's Law in any form."

"So you are looking at the sources of demand for the Gross National Product," Green inferred.

"Yes. Consumer demand by individuals, business investment in new capital equipment, government expenditure for items of collective consumption, and net exports."

"Then our present unemployment crisis is caused by inadequate consumer demand and inadequate business investment."

"That's correct," Sokolow declared.

"So you want to encourage consumption and investment."

"Right. There's not too much we can do about consumption because it depends on the level of income. Additional consumption will be brought about by income increases and will reinforce the increased demand."

"That's your multiplier effect," Green said.

"Yes, but to initiate the effect, we must look elsewhere."

"Can we get foreigners to buy more of our exports?"

"Not at the moment," Sokolow stressed. "Just like us, they are trying to export more and import less."

"That leaves private investment or government expenditure. And you are dubious about private investment," Green commented.

"Well, private investment often provides sufficient demand. But often it does not. I know of no mechanism that equates planned investment by business with savings intended by individuals at full-employment GNP."

"Doesn't the interest rate bring savings and investment together?" Green wanted to know.

"No, the interest rate depends mostly on supply and demand for money, not the tendency of people to save and invest."

"Then the interest rate is a monetary phenomenon?" Green said.

"Generally, yes, you could say that," Sokolow hedged. "Of course, you can make a model that reconciles———"

Green cut him short. "In the present circumstances, you

would increase the money supply to induce business to invest. Failing that, you would have the government make up the difference in demand."

"Yes!" Sokolow spoke almost violently.

"And you are not worried about inflation?"

"I'm worried about inflation, Admiral, but I see the need to increase output and employment. I believe that if we can increase output and employment, we will be able to deal with the immediate problem of inflation."

"And in the longer run?"

"Once we stem the panic, we will have greater output to match the demand. And we should come closer to full employment with limited inflation."

"But you don't expect to eliminate both unemployment and inflation, do you, Dr. Sokolow?"

"I think there is a trade-off between inflation and unemployment. The more we increase demand to combat unemployment, the greater will be the inflationary pressure as wages and other costs increase. The relationship between the two has been studied and charted by an economist named Phillips. The Phillips curve shows the inverse relationship between inflation and unemployment."

"Meaning that we have to choose between alternatives—how much more of one evil are we willing to bear in order to get less of the other?"

Sokolow answered slowly. "Only dreamers think they can have perfect equilibrium with no inflation or unemployment or misallocated resources. The Phillips curve only reflects the reality of an imperfect world."

"How do you know the Phillips curve is stable?"

"What do you mean by stable?"

"Well, it seems to me that the Phillips curve as you describe it should be reversible. If the authorities in a country decide that they want to go from a high-inflation and low-unemployment situation to one with lower inflation and somewhat higher unemployment, they should be able to do so. But it seems to me that the choices are continually getting worse. After each experience with inflation, we have to have a higher and higher rate of unemployment to get prices under control again."

Green further explained what he meant. "I think a good analogy would be to compare the trade-off between prices and inflation to the trade-off between the danger of infection from germs and the danger of allergic reaction to penicillin. The more doctors use penicillin, the more antibiotic-resistant varieties of bacteria develop. So it takes bigger and bigger doses of antibiotic to cure the same disease. The threat is that doctors would have to endanger patients more from the cure than from the disease itself—or the penicillin cure won't work at all."

"All right, Admiral, I see what you are saying," Sokolow conceded. "I agree with you up to a point. Each time we recover from a recession because the government guarantees employment by increasing demand, unions and firms become more convinced that they will always be bailed out and hence never lower their demands during slowdowns. The effect is sort of like a ratchet wrench—it turns only one way."

"Exactly. What can be done about it?"

"Well, we're in a tough situation. This world is in some ways more difficult than in the thirties, when expansionary fiscal and monetary policy had not been tried before."

"Like the world before penicillin?"

"Sure. The only thing I can say is that we are going to have to find ways to overcome the inflationary side effects. The government will have to use moral suasion. It is going to have to negotiate in situations where it will pressure firms and unions in key business sectors to moderate their demands to a level that can be accommodated by increased productivity. There are a bunch of other schemes, like tax incentives for moderation in price and wage demands, incentives to increase investment and productivity, and so on."

Green looked squarely at Sokolow. "All these measures you suggest show that there isn't going to be a *cure* for the present situation."

"For God's sake, what do you expect? No, there isn't going to be a cure—a miracle drug or policy that will wipe out economic disease and side effects for all time. There's going to be a constant pull and tug, adjustment and pressure, plan and direction. One way or another, we have to have a means of patching up the social contract that balances the various pressure groups and opposing interests in the country."

"Is that free enterprise?"

"Hell, no! Free enterprise was already a fiction in the nineteenth century. If it weren't for federal legislation and boondoggles in land—legal giveaways and illegal swindles—the West never would have been settled, the railroads never would have been built, the Indians never would have been successfully murdered. What the hell do you expect? For a practical man, a combat sailor, you sure are a dreamer if you expect complete victory with no casualties!"

Green ignored the virtual insult. He could not afford injured feelings when he needed all the facts he could get and needed them quickly. He made his own summing up. "I guess the difference between you and the monetarists is that they are perpetually hankering for a world of long-run adjustment. They resist any short-run policy that runs counter to the long-run goals they have set. You Keynesians think the long run is a dream, and are forever going to be adjusting the short run as best you can."

"I guess that's an evenhanded way of putting it, Admiral. After all our talk, which do you think is the right way to go?"

"To tell the truth, I'm not sure."

"Make up your mind."

"I have to. After I talk with Christopherson."

Sokolow's face darkened. "Remember Keynes," he grated. *"In the long run we are all dead.* I hope you've got that point. Don't let Christopherson talk you out of it!"

Again Green shrugged off the slight. He allowed the discussion to run on until he realized that Sokolow was now only repeating himself. At that point, the admiral rose to his feet, thanked the chairman of the Council of Economic Advisers, and made his departure. Alice went with him.

8
Money Talks

When Harcourt Green and Alice Ritter emerged from the Old Executive Office Building, they found they had a little time before the four o'clock appointment with Martin Christopherson at the Fed. They decided to walk.

"Sokolow sure is convinced he's right," Green said. "And he doesn't like anyone to disagree with him!"

"He thinks if you don't take his advice, you'll make the crisis worse than it already is," she replied.

"That's my problem. I don't know if he's right or wrong. Well, he gave me something to chew on. I just hope I don't get indigestion. Now, let's see what Christopherson has to say."

They walked along Constitution Avenue, ruminating over the situation, and turned in at the headquarters of the Federal Reserve System. It was a marble megalith, white, rectangular, austere, set back from the Constitution Avenue sidewalk. Its facade was decorated with bronze stars.

The two visitors were escorted to the chairman's office, which bore no resemblance to Sokolow's. The cliché forced itself on Alice's mind the moment she crossed the threshold: "A place for everything and everything in its place." No scattered papers, no piles of books—a clean desk.

Martin Christopherson was in his early forties. His tall, powerful physique matched his strongly chiseled features. He had been a middleweight boxer and had served on river patrol boats in Vietnam. On being discharged from the navy, he went to graduate school at the University of Chicago. He became a brilliant advocate of the monetarist position. It was not long before Christopherson followed his graduate adviser into a research position with the Federal Reserve Bank of Saint Louis, an institution that generally followed the monetarist position. By the time President Curtin took over on a monetarist platform, it was almost inevitable that Christopherson would be called to head the Fed.

Christopherson retained his boxing instincts as well as his physique. He was deadly in debate. His style was that of the counter-puncher. Controlled, contained, disarmingly plausible in verbal combat, he was known for his ability to lead his opponents on and then crush them with a sudden verbal blow.

The chairman of the Fed was the opposite of Sokolow in thought and style. Yet the same intensity was there. It simply expressed itself in the restrained world of the banking business, rather than in the informality of American college life.

Christopherson returned Green's handshake firmly. Green introduced his aide. "This is Lieutenant Alice Ritter. She knows something about economics. She'll have some input into the discussion." The banker acknowledged the young woman with a courtly bow. He invited his guests to take a couple of easy chairs while he sat behind his desk.

Green spoke first. "Mr. Christopherson, to pick up where we left off at the White House, I would like to have your assessment of the present emergency."

Christopherson rested his elbows on the arms of his swivel chair and made a pyramid with his fingers. "Our fundamental problems, Admiral Green, stem from three causes. We have lost control of the money supply, and this has given us inflation. We have not had a consistent policy toward inflation, so other governments believe our spasmodic efforts to control inflation will be followed by more inflationary episodes undermining the value of the dollar. And, we have lost our faith in the abilty of the market to direct resources to their most efficient use at full-employment levels. Everything else that has happened is really the working out of these three failures."

Green probed further. "That's all very general. Presumably these problems have existed for some time. What has brought on the present loss of confidence in the dollar?"

"Really, Admiral, isn't it obvious what has happened?"

"You tell me." Green detested having one question answered with another.

"Dr. Murray Sokolow is what has happened."

"Is that fair? Anyone can see you don't agree with Dr. Sokolow, but don't you think blaming all our troubles on one man is a bit much?"

"It isn't Murray Sokolow as a person, but what he stands for that's causing the crisis. The market knows that Sokolow is the ghost of John Maynard Keynes come back from the dead to haunt us. Sokolow stands for abandonment of control of the money supply, and that means rampant inflation."

"That's Wall Street's feeling now?"

"Yes, it is, and rightly so, because inflation is everywhere a monetary phenomenon. Notice it's not just Wall Street. The international markets are linked so closely by computers and electronic transactions that we are talking about a worldwide financial judgment."

Green objected, "But didn't the Fed at your order dramatically increase the money supply during the stock market meltdown of '87?"

"Yes, that's so," Christopherson conceded. "We had no choice but to make credit easier, to prevent the financial system from collapsing along with the stock market. The Fed had to give banks enough credit reserves so they could lend during the emergency. Actually, extending credit was a defense of the money supply, which otherwise would have collapsed as in 1932."

"So you are opposed," Green suggested, "to a contraction in the money supply that might lead to a depression."

"Exactly," Christopherson said. "That's what happened during the thirties. In any case, there is no comparison between an emergency measure for a few days or weeks, and Sokolow's determination to open the money faucet as a means of solving our problems. That just means inflation, despite the fine talk about a social contract to hold prices down."

He seemed about to say more, but Green got a point in first.

"That's very different from the explanation of the value of money implied by Dr. Sokolow. According to him, at least during a depression, wages are fixed by custom as 'money illusion,' and prices of everything are linked to the wage costs of production. Since the value of money is really inversely related to the price of everything else, Sokolow would have it that 'money illusion' in the wage bargain is what determines the value of money.

"But you believe," Green pursued the point, "that the price level depends on the quantity of money?"

Christopherson scowled. "There you have a critical difference. As I understand it, money is a form of wealth that performs certain functions as we buy and sell, store our wealth in liquid form, and the like. I don't believe in any fixed tie of money to the wage rate."

"It follows that the value of money is given by the laws of supply and demand like any other commodity," Green said.

"Sure. The increase in the supply of money reduces its value. That means raising the price of everything else, just as we said."

"What of the demand for money?"

"The demand for *real* money is stable. People only need money to buy other things. But real money—money supply corrected for price changes—has to have a real value. Inflation undermines that value. In fact, if people believe that dollars will not serve to store their wealth in liquid form, they will switch to other currencies that will do better."

Alice Ritter joined the conversation. "People protect themselves from inflation by turning their dollars into other valuables. And the financial markets reflect this fact."

Christopherson clasped his fingers together and nodded to show he appreciated her understanding of the problem.

"That accounts for the international flight from the dollar," he explained, "as people try to convert their dollars into other currencies they think are more stable. In plain English, the bottom has fallen out of the dollar market. I could put it more bluntly and say that fools have knocked the bottom out. I mean the Keynesians."

"What if other currencies do no better than ours?" Green queried.

"People will switch to other commodities."

"Such as?" Green prompted him.

"Such as gold, silver, diamonds, copper, grain, coal, stocks, real estate, railroad cars, nylons, cigarettes."

"So the prices of these things are rising because people are trying to get away from money they think will be worthless?"

"No doubt about it. And the reason the dollar is worth less is that Sokolow is hell-bent to increase the supply of dollars relative to the demand. He thinks he'll get lower interest rates, but he won't. He can't and he won't!"

Green held up a hand to stem Christopherson's flow of words. "Wait a minute. Before we get into that, I thought you were in charge of the money supply, not the Council of Economic Advisers or even the President of the United States. The Fed is organized as an independent agency, isn't it? You don't strike me as the sort of man who gives in easily."

"You give me too much credit," the banker said. "There are political realities to be faced even though the Fed is legally independent. If the President decides to follow Sokolow's advice, he is going to get his way sooner or later. He can appoint new members to the Board of Governors when terms expire or members resign or are seduced away to other positions."

"Congress can take a hand, too," Alice volunteered.

"Certainly. The Federal Reserve System is the creature of the Federal Reserve Act of 1913. The act can always be amended."

"The best you can do, then," she continued, "is to resist Sokolow and try your best to keep the President from using his leverage to make you change policies."

"Or forcing me to resign and replacing me with someone who will do what Sokolow wants," Christopherson added.

"And you don't want to resign." Green made it sound like a statement rather than a question.

"No, I don't want to resign. Don't misunderstand me. I don't hanker after this job. Lord knows, it doesn't pay half of what a senior banker can earn in the private sector."

"Still, it gives you power no private banker has."

"That's true. But this job is one of conflicting pressures. When you need the power to discipline governments as well as businesses, it slips away from you. Admiral, you've been in Washington long enough to understand that."

Green expressed his agreement with a shrug.

"I need to do my duty, just as you need to do yours," the chairman exclaimed.

"And Dr. Sokolow needs to do his," Alice commented.

"We all defend our country when it is a matter of life or death, as it is now," Christopherson responded sharply.

Green rubbed a thumb along his jaw. "Christopherson, how far would you go in defending the country?"

"As far as you, Green."

The reply intrigued Green so much that he decided to press the point. "Do you mean you would take human lives to control the money supply?"

Christopherson scowled at him. "Didn't we take lives to control coral atolls in the Pacific? Control of the money supply is much more crucial to national safety than any rock out in the South Seas!"

Neither Harcourt Green nor Alice Ritter had any doubt that Martin Christopherson meant exactly what he said.

"But it hasn't come to that," the chairman added in a relaxed tone. "Has it? Unless we decide to solve our economic problems by going to war."

The conversation had taken such a curious turn that the three fell silent. Then Green cocked a finger at the banker as if it were a pistol. "A few minutes ago," he said, "you identified loss of control of the money supply as the first cause of the crisis that threatens the national safety. And you blame Sokolow."

"Not forgetting the others over there at the Council of Economic Advisers."

"Is the President at fault for appointing Sokolow?"

"Yes."

"And me for listening to him?"

"I wouldn't say that. You have to hear everybody out. But

it's your responsibility to make up your mind in a way that will save the nation from disaster."

"What if I make it up wrong?"

"I hope you won't!" Christopherson pounded a fist in the palm of his hand. "Don't go the Sokolow route! If you do, we're all in trouble! And you'll be responsible!"

Alice decided they were getting too angry. She tried to intervene as a peacemaker.

"Forget it, Lieutenant," the Admiral commanded. "I think this man is threatening me!"

The banker frowned. "I was only trying to express my confidence in your judgment. You're not going to be taken in by Sokolow and the soft-headed crowd that thinks the government can repair all the evils of society by tossing money around."

Green was only slightly mollified. He stuck to his guns. "Nevertheless, I can see the force of Sokolow's argument. He is concerned with high interest rates. He tells me that at the present rates, firms will not invest in new equipment, the housing industry will continue in a state of collapse, and agriculture will face bankruptcy. There's a lot in that, if you ask me."

Christopherson was ready. "The question is, how do you get interest rates down? Sokolow says that lower interest rates can be achieved by increasing the money supply. He thinks supply and demand for money is adjusted through some equilibrating interest rate, while I am saying that supply and demand for money determines the value of money."

"You mean the price of everything else when you say the value of money?" Green inferred.

"Right! By increasing the money supply we will raise the present price level and increase expectations about future price levels. Then interest rates will rise rather than fall."

"But," Alice said, "increasing the money supply is done by the Fed in the open market. Buying bonds increases the reserves of banks when they are paid by the Fed, but it raises the price of bonds. That means a lower interest rate."

Christopherson drummed his fingertips on the top of his

desk. "Only in the short run and in short-term debt where inflation is not so important. It's true that each time we buy bonds, we increase the money supply and push interest rates down. But we also fuel inflation, which drives interest rates up. If we keep on increasing the money supply as Sokolow wants us to, we will be forever raising the rate of inflation by pouring more money into the market. In the long run, interest rates will go up and up, and the country will go straight to hell!"

"So the issue is whether the main impact of changes in the money supply is on the price level as you say, or on the rate of interest as Sokolow says," Alice reasoned.

The banker nodded. "Allowing for a time lag, there is a direct relationship between the price level and the money supply."

"Even under conditions of unemployment?" Green asked.

"That's what the evidence shows," Christopherson stressed.

"But during the Great Depression, didn't prices go down even though the money supply increased?"

"Not so! I deny that! Prices started to fall at the onset of the Depression in '29 because the Federal Reserve reacted to the panic by allowing the money supply to contract."

"You didn't make that mistake during the October '87 crash?" Green asked.

"No, we did not. But in the thirties, constantly increasing the money supply became an article of Keynesian faith. Then, after a lag, prices began to rise, just as they would now."

"With a lag? How long is your lag in these situations?"

"It varies. Say two years."

"Two years!" Green was on his feet and pacing. "Mr. Banker, I have been charged by the President of the United States to recommend policy decisions to be taken Sunday afternoon. I ask for your advice, and you recommend policies that will take two years to work!"

Christopherson counterpunched. "There's no free lunch. If we're going to control inflation, we'll have to think in long-run terms. We're in this bind because the politicians were so preoccupied with short-run effects that they didn't think about the long run. But it's here now, just as everybody at the Fed said it would be, regardless of the variations in their economic theories."

"Sorry, I lost my temper," Green apologized, but he glanced at his watch before sitting down again. His patience with these economists was wearing thin. His training had not prepared him for their abstractions, their contradictory appeals to the same evidence, or their dogmatism.

"We operate on what is sometimes called a paper-money standard," Christopherson said in a less challenging tone.

"I wouldn't brag about that fact, if I were you."

"Well, I don't like the phrase either. Still, money retains its value through supply and demand for it, representing as it does the debt of the government."

"I understand that. It's an uncollectable debt, too, isn't it?"

Christopherson refused to be baited. "The easiest way to see the point is to express the value of goods sold————"

"Gross National Product?" Green interrupted.

"Roughly. The value of goods transacted is equal to the price of the average good."

"The price level?"

"Yes. The value of goods is equal to the price of the average good multiplied by the number of goods."

"GNP equals P times Q where P is the price level and Q is the number of goods produced. We engineering people like to think algebraically," Green commented.

"I am aware of your training and accomplishments in scientific matters," said Christopherson dryly.

"Go on, please. Now you're making sense."

"Well then, the value of goods sold can be expressed also as the quantity of money in existence multiplied by the number of times it is used, or turned over, in a year. Call the number of turnovers the velocity of money."

"So, algebraically again, the Gross National Product is equal to M times V, where M is the quantity of money and V is the velocity of money."

"As you must be thinking, Admiral, MV equals PQ."

Green slipped a notebook from his pocket and wrote down

the equation. "The quantity of money," he said, "multiplied by the number of times it is used in a year is equal to the price of the average commodity multiplied by the number of commodities. And both sides of the equation equal the GNP."

"Yes," Christopherson agreed.

"All right, now tell me your theory."

"Very well." Christopherson swiveled to one side in his chair and launched into his discourse. "The value of a dollar bill is nothing but one dollar divided by the price of other things. So if we measured the value of dollars in, say, tuna fish, one dollar divided by the price of tuna fish would be the number of cans of tuna fish a dollar would buy."

Green chuckled. "I know the Fed has given up on gold, but are you really measuring GNP in tuna fish these days?"

Christopherson smiled. "Well, that's one example. That's why we divide one dollar by the average price of all goods, the price level, to get the true value of the dollar bill. So if we know what determines the price level, we know the value of money. Okay?"

Green nodded. "If prices go up, the value of money goes down, and vice versa."

"But the price level is M times V divided by Q. In plain English, the price level equals the quantity of money times its velocity divided by the quantity of goods transacted."

Green agreed. "Of course, the value of all the goods in the aggregate divided by the number of goods gives the price of the average good."

The banker went on. "So the price level is proportional to the quantity of money. If M goes up on one side of the equation, P must go up on the other side *by the same percentage.*"

Green was struck by a problem. "An increase in M brings on an increase in P only if Q and V are constants."

"But they are—in the long run," Christopherson stated.

"How long? Two years?"

"It could be. It's important to see why. In the long run, the economy tends to full employment, less perhaps the natural rate of unemployment that arises from the frictions and mismatches in the labor market. That means that Q is given by the number of employees, and the gradual accumulation of capital, and the supply of natural resources they have to work with."

"And what about V?" Green inquired.

"The velocity of money depends on the amount of it that people hold. That doesn't change much because money is just a means to an end."

"I suppose so—nobody eats money. Green spoke satirically.

Christopherson was not perturbed. "So the velocity of money expresses the stable ratio of the convenient amount of cash people have on hand relative to the value of goods they are going to buy."

"You are leading me, Mr. Banker, but I think you're saying this: Firms hire more workers because an increase in M times the stable V means an increase in the demand for GNP." Green gestured impatiently. "In the short run, your description of what happens if the money supply increases is roughly the same as Sokolow's description of the increase in employment resulting from greater government spending."

Christopherson could not contain himself. "That's nonsense, Admiral! An increase in the money supply takes three to nine months to affect employment. So you don't get a quick fix. Besides, the effect of that increase in employment wears off, and turns into an increase in prices rather than output."

"But in the short run——" Green started to say.

Christopherson cut him off. "To hell with the short run!" The banker's decorum had vanished. "What are you going to do in nine months when employment starts to slow down again? Raise the money supply some more? Inflate some more? Goddammit, Green, you're supposed to face reality. We have to stop this runaway inflation now."

Alice spoke calmly. "And face the consequences, now, of bankruptcies and mass unemployment?"

"That's the price we have to pay, like it or not," the banker retorted. "If we don't pay it now, we will later on down the line. And it will be a thousand times worse."

Alice persisted. "That would be the choice, Mr. Christopherson, if we were sure about the velocity of money. Does the evidence prove it's constant?"

Green shot an appreciative look at his aide. He had seen Sokolow's defense of the liquidity trap falter when confronted by actual numbers, and he wondered if this constant velocity would fare any better.

Christopherson took up the challenge. "Well, I don't maintain that the velocity is a constant, only that the demand for real inflation-adjusted cash balances is stable. If we know how much cash people want to hold in bank balances at any time, we can figure how fast money must be moving."

Green would not let Christopherson off. He followed Alice Ritter's lead. "Okay, is the demand for real money constant?"

"No. But it's in a stable relationship to the wealth of a country and interest rates."

Green plunged in. "Oh boy! I just heard from Sokolow that the demand for liquid cash depends on the interest rate. I don't see you as very different."

The banker spoke angrily. "No! No! I don't say that interest rates won't affect the demand for money. I only deny that there is such a thing as a liquidity trap. There cannot be such an unlimited demand for cash that no matter how much is available, lenders refuse to cut interest rates. The demand for money cannot be infinite—people don't go crazy and out of panic hold everything they own in cash. That's what we're driving at when we talk about stable demand for money.

Alice spoke again. "Well, if your equation of exchange is to work in explaining prices————"

"And therefore the value of money," Green interjected. He was on the same wavelength with his aide.

Alice repeated his words. "And therefore the value of money." Then she went on. "If so, the velocity of money can't jump around all over the place. Has that been the case recently?"

Green echoed her thought. "Has it?"

"Historically————" Christopherson began, but Green was not interested.

61

"The most important thing about history is that it's over," the admiral jabbed. "Has the demand for money been stable recently?"

"In these last years," Christopherson conceded, "the velocity of money has not been stable." Then he went over to the offensive. "Nevertheless, you can't ignore history, Admiral. Playing with variations in the money supply to solve problems is like Russian roulette. Sooner or later the money demand number will come up."

Christopherson did not mention that he was being criticized at the Federal Reserve by the "new classical economists." For them, history was indeed over. The monetarist reliance on past behavioral patterns of habit, rather than rational expectations of the future, seemed too close to Keynesian notions.

Just now, the Federal Reserve chairman stuck to his guns. "Your question, Admiral, is debated within the Fed. But anybody who attempts to use some statistical difficulties in our projections to start inflation all over again is going to do so over my dead body!"

There was silence for a moment. Then Christopherson went on. "You know, Admiral, it may just be that too much is being asked of us at the Fed. We may control the money supply, but we don't make the spending and taxing decisions that determine the deficit. Afterward, we are called on to solve problems we didn't create."

Green was understanding. "You face real dilemmas over here."

"We sure do. We're asked to hold down interest rates at the same time as the Treasury is borrowing money to finance federal spending. We are asked to increase the money supply so banks can lend, and at the same time, we're asked to hold down inflation by restricting the money supply."

"There are limits to what monetary policy can do."

"Yes, of course. There is no cure-all."

Green had heard that before, and decided to change the subject. He brought up an issue on which Sokolow had placed much emphasis. "What about the Phillips curve? The trade-off between inflation and unemployment?"

The chairman of the Fed grimaced and shook his head. "I can see you've been talking to Sokolow. There is no such thing as a Phillips curve, at least in the long run."

Green was flabbergasted. "What do you mean? There are rates of inflation and rates of unemployment. Didn't this fellow Phillips plot them on a graph and connect the points and . . ."

"And what? Do the points all lie on a nice curve?"

"No, the curve shifts. Sokolow admitted that to me when I questioned him."

"Not to be impolite, Admiral, but you may not have questioned him as strenuously as you are interrogating me. After all, does anybody really observe a curve when you plot those inflation-unemployment points?"

"You tell me."

Christopherson did so, emphatically. "You observe a scatter of points, and you have to say whether those points lie on a curve. The points don't say it for you. You have a mishmash of inflation and unemployment points all over the place for recent years. You could say they lie on a gyrating curve, or that there is no curve. You pay your money and you take your choice."

"Then why do the Keynesians believe in the Phillips curve when it may or may not exist?" Alice wondered.

"There are two reasons. First of all, it's a necessity for them theoretically to explain the price level. In the Keynesian system, the price level depends on the money wage rate, which itself is really not explained."

"Not in the long run," Alice replied. "But in the short run, the Keynesians think wages are a given—by habit or tradition—as 'money illusion,' to use their phrase."

"That's just an excuse for no explanation at all," Christopherson declared. "The idea of sticky, unchanging wages makes no sense now in an era of inflation, if it ever made sense during the Great Depression."

"So they invented something else," Green suggested.

"Exactly. The Keynesians replaced sticky wages based on fixed illusions with this Phillips curve in which the wage rate and the price level are said to be determined by the rate of unemployment."

"And what is the second reason?" Green pressed him.

"The second reason is that the Keynesian policy hasn't worked. It has *not* solved the problem of unemployment because, in the long run at least, *unemployment is given by the natural rate of unemployment.* We have the same unemployment and more inflation. To explain it away, the Sokolow people talk of a shifting Phillips curve. It's a phony."

"There is no trade-off between inflation and unemployment?"

"Not in the long run," Christopherson declared.

"What the hell!" Green could take only so much of this long-run and short-run game. "All right, is there a short-run Phillips curve?"

Christopherson shrugged. "I guess you could say there is a semblance of one. When prices rise, wages tend to lag behind."

"Due to money illusion, I suppose." Green could not resist the sly reference to Sokolow's theory.

Christopherson remained unperturbed, at least on the surface. "The point is that when prices rise and wages lag behind, then the real cost of labor falls and employers get higher profits. They are motivated to hire more workers. Thus, in the short run, inflation results in less unemployment than the natural rate that holds in the long run."

"Is the long run relevant at all?" Green demanded.

The banker became insistent. "It certainly is—because when wages catch up to the new price level, the temporary incentive to hire extra workers disappears. Unemployment necessarily rises again."

"Then tell me what you believe. Forget all the statistics and give me your gut feeling."

Christopherson shrugged. "I believe people look at realities—real wages, real interest rates, real income. They are not victims of any kind of money illusion for very long. Five million dollars for a navy fighter plane is a lot of money only because it is a million times more expensive than a five-dollar movie ticket. The real price of that plane is a ratio to the prices of other things."

The banker appeared to be organizing his ideas in the most effective order before he continued. "Relative prices are not affected by the money supply for long periods of time. The market system gets us to relative prices by the process of supply and demand.

"While changes in the money supply can cause nominal price changes, they have real effects only in the short run when the ratios have not worked themselves out. For instance, in the long run, the labor market clears because of real wage adjustments to the price of goods—except for the frictional elements that make up the natural rate of unemployment. The nominal or money wage has an effect only if there is a lag in adjustment."

Green tapped a knuckle against his chin and looked doubtful. Christopherson took this as the moment to press his theme before it was lost on his listeners. "I think that when people decide how much money to hold, they are concerned with real money."

"I believe you. They are not concerned about fake money," Green snorted.

"Look, Admiral, this is not a joke. People are not concerned about the nominal amount of their cash balances—the number of pieces of green paper or numbers in the checking account—but what they can buy with these pieces of paper. They are looking at their real cash balances. If the government increased the money supply in nominal terms, it would not change a thing. People would hold the same real cash balances, adjusted for inflation. Therefore, the amount of real money they would spend would be the same, but the nominal money spent would be higher and so would prices."

"The amount of goods demanded would be unaffected?"

"Certainly. Think of that equation of exchange we talked about earlier, MV equals PQ. You could say the same thing, in terms of real money, by dividing both sides by P. Then you would have M divided by P, the money supply corrected for inflation to give us the real money supply, times V, the velocity of money. You can see that real money times velocity would be equal to Q, the real quantity of goods produced."

"Then the heart of your belief," Alice said, "is that the amount of goods is unaffected by the money supply, since only real magnitudes matter to rational people?"

"In the long run," the admiral prodded the chairman.

"In the long run, dammit. Don't knock it, Admiral. It's economic reality. Act on my advice, and the American people will thank you one day. Act on Sokolow's advice, and you will be remembered as the man who contributed to an American tragedy. You can't say I didn't warn you."

"No, I can't, Christopherson. Well, I've had about as much economics as I can stand just now. We might as well break up. I'll give everything you've said my full attention between now and Sunday."

A couple of minutes later the admiral and his aide were back on Constitution Avenue.

Inside the marble building, Christopherson was saying into the telephone, "Yes, I know it's hard for you to mix business with pleasure." A female voice on the other end was petulant, but Christopherson persisted. "Yes, yes, it *is* a difficult matter, I agree, but I will make it worth your while." The voice over the telephone seemed less resistant. "Double what I paid last time," Christopherson promised. "This is most urgent."

The reply was not audible beyond the receiver, but the voice at the other end seemed to acquiesce. Christopherson was pleased. "Good, thank you," he said. "You won't be sorry. Good-bye."

9

A Tryst

"Time for us to quit," Green said. "I'll drop you at your apartment and go on home."

He hailed a taxi and they drove through Washington to the building where Alice lived. The admiral escorted the lieutenant to the door, bade her good night, returned to the taxi, and gave the driver the next address.

In her room, Alice glanced out the front window. She was just in time to see the taxi turn around and head back in the opposite direction. "He's going to Georgetown," she thought, "to visit his blonde. I wonder what Marianne will say to him!"

Alice dialed a number. When she got her connection, she spoke one word: "Georgetown."

Preoccupied with his own thoughts, Green did not notice a compact car that pulled out of a side street and followed the taxi at a discreet distance. Much less did it register with him that his wife was driving the car. Frances Green tailed the taxi all the way to Marianne's address, an elegant, two-story town-house, remodeled and divided, like so many Georgetown residences, into fashionable apartments.

After watching her husband unlock the front door and go in as she cruised past, Frances picked up speed and headed for home at a rapid clip.

Green mounted the stairs to the second floor and reached Marianne's door. He was fumbling for his key when the door opened and Marianne van Thuys stood in the doorway. She held one hand on the doorknob and the other on her hip where her crimson silk dress was cleverly shaped to conceal a tendency toward plumpness. The color flattered the creamy tones of her skin and contrasted effectively with streaked blonde hair caught back from her face and coiled at the nape of her neck.

Several long gold chains hung around her neck, reflecting the color of her hair. A marquise diamond adorned her finger. She looked elegant and self-assured—as though she had taken the world's measure and could cope with it.

Marianne welcomed Green with easy familiarity and closed the door behind him. Her apartment was a mixture of Continental and Indonesian styles that reflected her childhood in Java. Her father, Jost van Thuys, had been one of the Dutch engineers invited to help expand the electrical industry that was part of the newly independent country's postwar development plan. Van Thuys stayed for three years, implementing as far as he could the government's plan for industrializing the economy. It ended as a frustrating failure. The design that most of the projects called for did not suit local conditions. Van Thuys had been asked to introduce the latest technology, yet the basic requirements for high-technology industry were not in place. There was little skilled labor, the power supply was uncertain, and roads and transport were inadequate. Worst of all, the bureaucracy stymied all attempts at experimentation and innovation.

The van Thuys family returned to Holland, but like so many Dutch they took with them a deep affection for Javanese culture. Marianne's apartment centered on a low teak table surrounded by sofas and cushions. Hot satie sticks of meat were grilling on charcoal in the table insert, ready to be dipped in aromatic peanut sauce.

"I have the Armagnac, Harry," she said in her Dutch-accented English.

Green allowed her to undo his tie and push him down on the sofa. Marianne handed him the brandy glass. Sitting on the low cushion opposite, she crossed her ankles under her and waited.

Green sat silently and emptied the glass. Marianne refilled it. She lit a small cigar and studied Green's solemn face through the smoke.

"Something is bothering you. Is it Frances?"

"Yes, Marianne. She knows about us."

"That doesn't surprise me. Does it surprise you?"

Green shrugged. "I thought she might find out some day. Just how, well, it never occurred to me."

Marianne tapped the ash from her cigar into an ashtray. "Wives can put two and two together."

"All right! But she had me shadowed by a private detective. I never thought she'd stoop so low. We had a real row about it. She was simmering when I left the house. So was I. And I don't know how it's all going to work out."

"Divorce?"

The admiral grimaced. "I think we love each other too much for that, although I must say I was shocked by her attitude today. I've never seen her in such a temper before. I thought she was ready to shoot me. Which reminds me, I'd better phone her."

Marianne gave him a sympathetic look. "You are a husband complaining about his wife to his mistress. Do you really want to do that, darling?"

"No, of course not."

"Maybe we should stop seeing each other."

"No! Seeing you helps me more than anything. The truth is that Frances exasperates me because she knows me too well. She knows about us and I think she knows what you mean to me. But I doubt if anyone else does."

Marianne refilled their glasses. Green held his up to the light and inspected the color.

"The point is that my personal affairs don't count just now when the country is in trouble. I have to help the President make a major decision on Sunday. I really can't say more than that. The issues are very delicate and difficult."

He picked up the phone and dialed his home. The maid answered.

"Mrs. Green went out. She said she was going shopping."

Green felt relieved that he did not have to talk to Frances. "When she gets back, tell her I've got a late-night session at the

White House. I can't get away. I'll sleep in the office and see her tomorrow." He hung up.

Marianne continued her talk. "Decisions are nothing new for you, Harry. You have always been able to make up your mind and take the consequences or the glory."

"That's kind of you, Marianne. The truth is, though, that I have always had a gut feeling for the right course of action in military or strategic political matters. Those hunches come with experience."

"But now . . . ?"

"Now I have to make decisions about an issue in which I have very little background. Worse yet, there are two opposing—and reasonable—points of view that I have to negotiate between."

"And so you need some time and peace of mind to think it through."

"Yes."

"And Frances does not provide peace of mind?"

"Frances rarely permits peace of mind. She and her oddball friends! Now, well, I don't even know what she'll be like when I get home. I want to forget her tonight. I want to get my mind settled so I can think clearly."

"And so you are here."

"Yes."

Marianne turned the skewers of the satie. She removed the meat from the skewers and dipped the pieces in the peanut sauce before putting the plate of food in Harry's hands. Green allowed himself to be waited on.

She was not so much a beautiful woman as an arresting one. No longer very young, Marianne van Thuys thought of herself in terms of the men she attracted and enthralled. In place of youth there was an elegance of dress and grooming of face, hands, and figure that expressed her understanding of herself and her role in a world of men.

By midnight the tension was gone from Green's face. He momentarily put out his hand and touched her fingertips lightly. Marianne needed men like Harcourt Green. She needed

70

them needing her. It was their need, the need to talk as well as love, that gave her a feeling of not quite power, nor anything as psychological as self-worth, but rather a justified existence.

The aroma of the satie mingled with the smoke. Marianne filled Harry's glass once more and poured for herself. They toasted one another. She moved to his side. And then, taking him by the hand, she led him into the bedroom. Two brandy glasses were left on the table near the charcoal. The red flame glowed under the coating of ashes.

Green awoke to find himself alone in Marianne's bed. Quickly he dressed and walked out into the kitchen, where a small table was set for two. Marianne poured strong black coffee into small cups. The table was set in Dutch fashion, with rolls and thin slices of ham and cheese.

It was before summer dawn, but four hours' sleep had refreshed the admiral. He had never lost his sailor's habit of adjusting his physiological clock to the four-hour-watch schedule at sea. It gave him that much more time to work and to plan while others were dead to the world.

"Have you been asleep?" he asked Marianne.

She shook her head. "Women are not made sleepy by spent passion, you know. It's one of our virtues."

He inhaled the aroma rising from the coffee pot. He sipped his coffee, studying the woman across the table. "What have you been doing?"

"Reading. The papers are full of the financial crisis. The press reports that Monday morning will see a massive flight from the dollar as soon as Wall Street opens."

"Marianne, what do you know about international finance?"

"Admiral Green, do you think that Jost van Thuys's daughter is without experience in money and international financial maneuvering?"

"I mean it's so . . ." Harry groped for the right word.

". . . masculine. Do you think I am of the masculine or feminine gender, Admiral?"

Harry grinned at her over the coffee cup.

"Darling, when I was a little girl, I learned my ABC's—how

to take your money out of country A and get it into country B before moving it along to country C. More than that, I learned why and when to do it. How do you think the van Thuys family survived wars, revolutions, inflations, and financial panics?"

Green settled his coffee cup on the table. "Tell me, Marianne, what does Jost van Thuys's daughter make of the economy now?"

"Harry, darling, if you are asking how I manage my money, it is really none of your business. You possess me, but not my money."

"No, you misunderstand . . ."

"Can it be true that the great Admiral Harcourt Green is looking for financial advice from a Dutch woman?"

"Stop teasing, Marianne. I'm serious."

"Then what do you want to know, Harry?"

"I want to know what people like you—foreigners, people with an international viewpoint—make of the present economic situation in the United States."

"All right, Harry. In one respect, the United States is not much different from any other country I have lived in. Every once in a while, governments get grandiose ideas about spending more money than they can afford. There are all kinds of reasons for that. Most often it has to do with armaments—the little boys who run the world like to play soldier. Sometimes governments get involved in commitments to spend money simply to prevent unemployment. In some of the less-developed countries, governments get involved in all kinds of overblown development plans. They build steel mills, harbors, and fancy airports. They dedicate marble capitals in the middle of the jungle, naming them after their leaders."

"And then?"

"Then, Harry darling, they run the printing presses and produce more and more paper money."

"They could tax . . ."

"Harry, for a tough-minded naval strategist you're awfully

naïve when it comes to the politics of money. I don't know whether most governments *could* tax enough for their fancy ideas, or even if they *should* tax to get their great plans carried out, but I do know they *won't* tax. Everywhere the van Thuys family has been in this world, governmental schemes are financed by making more and more paper money."

"And . . ."

"And the result is that when there is so much money around it becomes worthless. Usually prices rise as people try to buy scarce goods with money that is not scarce at all."

"Inflation."

"Yes, inflation is always related to money in my experience. More money means the value of money goes down, and that means higher prices. Inflation is everywhere a monetary phenomenon, even though governments try to find somebody to blame like OPEC or the trade unions."

"I suppose you're saying that labor costs and petroleum costs are the effects of inflation, not the cause."

Marianne brought more coffee and filled Green's cup. She sat next to him and put a fresh helping of rolls and ham on his plate. "You know, the men who run the world cannot face up to the fact that when they stub their toe it's their own fault. They have to blame somebody else. Women know that. That's why they make allowances for what men do."

"Well, let's stick to economics. In your international experience, what usually happens if inflation continues?"

"Then the money becomes worth less and less, and people find other things to invest in. You know, chocolates, nylons, cigarettes . . ."

"Or diamonds or gold or silver."

"Yes, goods instead of the empty promises of governments. Sooner or later governments end up repudiating their debts. Some strong man—a dictator, usually—says that the old money is worthless and must be traded in for new money at a discount. Then anyone stuck with the old money takes a beating."

"And the van Thuys family?"

"The van Thuys family gets rid of that kind of money before it becomes worthless."

"That only drives the value of money down further, causing more inflation."

"Harry, dear, do you want me to try to hold back inflation single-handed or to survive? I am only one woman standing against the follies of men in high places."

Green laughed. "No, I don't expect that you'll try to save the world."

"Just myself, Harry. Just myself."

Green finished his cup and stood up, ready to leave. Marianne stood with him. Then he said, "Tell me one more thing. You've lumped together various kinds of government expenditures, as if they all involved paying paper money for goods that otherwise would go to the private sector of the economy. Suppose government expenditure puts to work labor and other resources that would otherwise remain unemployed."

"Then what happens, Harry?"

"Then the effect of government spending is to increase output and employment even as it might increase the money supply. I have been hearing a lot of that lately."

"That is the silly way some people talk. You asked about the van Thuys family. We're not dreamers about a world of if and maybe and wait for the roof to fall in."

"Might it not work that way? Maybe we could escape from unemployment without necessarily causing inflation."

"Maybe, Harry. You know more than I, but my experience is that the effect of government spending is only to raise prices when it is not wasting resources."

"What do you think about unemployment?"

"Not much. I am sure there's a natural rate of unemployment that has to do with people being sick or women stuck at home with kids to raise and no husband to support them or people in temporary transit from one job to another—that sort of thing."

"What about mass unemployment, as in a depression?"

"I'm sure it's caused by the government tinkering with the money supply and creating so much uncertainty that businessmen back off. Apart from that kind of blundering, it seems to me that when people decide to take the wage the market will pay, they will always find work. If the government prints money it might give employment a temporary boost—a quick high—but soon it will just settle down to the same old natural rate of unemployment, accompanied by higher prices."

"You're a shrewd woman, Marianne. You've helped me more than you know. If it weren't for your practical good sense, I might still be floundering in a mess of academic abstractions."

Green looked at his watch. "Damn, I'll be late if I don't rush off." Marianne helped him with his coat, brushing a speck off the collar. They kissed and she saw him out of the apartment into the hall.

Marianne van Thuys closed the door behind her and settled into the couch. She picked up the telephone. The voice at the other end answered, "Federal Reserve, Mr. Christopherson's office."

The next voice, speaking in low confidential tones, became persistent in its questioning. Marianne answered somewhat petulantly, "Of course he didn't tell me explicitly what he's going to do. I'm not supposed to know. You know that."

Evidently the chairman of the Federal Reserve was not satisfied. Exasperated, Marianne replied, "I tell you he agrees with me. Look, he's not a stupid man. Everything does not have to be spelled out. Besides, if I press too hard, he might get his back up. I know how to deal with a man like him. A woman's touch is more effective than all your economic arguments."

Mollified, Christopherson permitted the conversation to close on her terms. In his office, he sat for a long time afterward at his desk staring out the window at the familiar Washington skyline of parks and monuments.

Marianne stretched luxuriantly. Then she headed for a perfumed bath and a nap. She had accomplished a great deal.

10
Stormy Weather

When Green got to his White House office, Alice Ritter was already there.

"I had the secretary type up the notes on the economy," she said, placing a sheaf of papers on his desk.

He refused to look her in the eye. "I intended to be here earlier, but I got caught in traffic."

The phone rang, and Green snatched it before Alice could. "I don't want any calls unless its urgent," he warned the operator.

"But Admiral Green, it's the President calling."

Hastily apologizing, Green heard Wedik's voice come on the line. "What's happening, Green? I'm cooped up on this tin can listening to John Ritter's soothing talk. What's happening? I heard there was a press leak in the *Wall Street Journal* about me being out of Washington."

The admiral suddenly realized he had been so completely absorbed by economics that he had all but forgotten the President, "such as he is," Green thought aloud.

"Such as what, Harry?" the voice on the telephone demanded.

"I'm sorry, Mr. President, I was just thinking. So much has happened————"

"What happened, Harry? What?"

"Nothing drastic, Mr. President. I've been trying to get a handle on the situation as you directed. I have lots of information and————"

"Come out to the *Chesapeake* and tell me about it, Harry."

"I'm all involved, sir————"

Wedik's voice rose a few decibels. "Well, get uninvolved, Green. I'm President of the United States and I want to know what's happening."

"Very well, Mr. President. I'll tell you all that I found out and————"

"Good, good. Come tonight before dinner. Bring your wife."

"Yes, sir."

"Bring that black girl, too."

"You mean Lieutenant Ritter?"

"Yes, yes. The daughter of the captain of this rust bucket. Her."

"Yes, sir."

Wedik was shouting so loudly that Alice, sitting next to the desk, heard plainly what the President said. She rose to her feet and mouthed the words, "I'll make the arrangements." She slipped out into her own office.

Green was trying to mollify Wedik. "Yes, Mr. President, sir. No, sir, I have not made any binding decisions for you. I would never do that!"

When Alice Ritter saw the telephone light flicker off she returned. "We can take the helicopter and land on deck in daylight, Admiral. The forecast is for some weather during the night."

"All right, Alice, arrange it. I'll call Frances."

"I've done that, Admiral. She'll be ready. I'm going to pick her up and drive back here to the helicopter. I thought you might need some time to work things out before you have to face the music."

As the door closed behind his aide, Green reached for the telephone and dialed a Georgetown number. Alice picked up her extension and listened. Silently she replaced the receiver as the conversation drew to a close.

Green strode through her office. "I'm going out, Alice. Don't worry, I'll be back in plenty of time to meet you and Mrs. Green here for the helicopter."

As the door closed, Alice dialed a number. Whatever was said on the other end was inaudible. She said only one word. "Georgetown."

Then she left the office and drove to the Green home. The expressway was relatively clear of traffic, so she made good time. Frances Green was at the portico, waiting. Alice thought that she had never seen the admiral's wife so preoccupied or uncommunicative. They exchanged a few words and went upstairs. Frances had not even started packing, but she did have a list of items she wanted to take with her to the ship. Together they fitted her clothing and toilet articles into a small, soft-sided travel bag. Frances Green had learned to travel light during the years of her husband's naval service.

The two went out to the car. Alice slid in under the wheel. She smoothed her uniform skirt and turned the key. The engine came to life.

Half an hour later they reached the White House. Admiral Green was waiting for them. Frances walked over to him, kissed his cheek, and took his arm. The three climbed aboard the waiting helicopter.

The navy pilot took off and they circled up over the White House grounds, heading toward Chesapeake Bay for their rendezvous with the presidential ship. The Treasury Building next door to the White House slipped away under the chopper almost immediately. So did the gewgawed Old Executive Office Building that housed the Council of Economic Advisers and Murray Sokolow. As the helicopter passed between the Washington Monument and the Lincoln Memorial, they could see the white, oblong headquarters of the Federal Reserve System, where Martin Christopherson held forth. The National Academy of Science next to it made Frances think of the statue of Albert Einstein. She had been on a committee to prevent the erection of the gilt, larger-than-life tribute to the father of relativity physics. Einstein was a man of reason and modesty. He neither wanted nor needed a golden likeness, but the protestors had been overruled, and the statue was there on the grounds of the academy.

The helicopter headed out to the open water where the President's ship was waiting for them. Alice did not like the accumulating gray on the horizon. She wondered if the radar on board the ship was picking up a storm.

The pilot settled the aircraft neatly on the landing pad aboard ship despite the slight pitch of the sea. Built toward the end of World War II, the ship had once been a light cruiser. No longer useful for combat service, it did provide a fairly secure sea base for the President. The gun turrets had been removed and replaced with a swimming pool and various sun decks, but the ship was capable of high speeds and was built of thicknesses of armored steel. Electronic communication and antimissile gear made it an easy place to arrange for presidential leisure and safety.

Even in the sheltered waters of Chesapeake Bay, the trio found themselves suddenly thrown into the world of the sea. The wind pressed their clothes to their bodies and brushed cold against their faces. The slight swells of the gray-green water were flecked with white froth where the wind sheared the tops of the wavelets. Everywhere there was motion: the slight pitch and roll of the ship, the vibration of the engines, the straining of the vessel against the pressure of the estuary current.

Chief Ritter came to the side of the helicopter as the engines were turned down. Tall and broad shouldered, he had a friendly smile and a sailor's squint and rolling gait. Green grasped the hand of his former shipmate, and they handed the two women down onto the deck. With the rush of cool sea air and the presence of his old comrade in arms, the admiral felt revived and able to cope with the fearsome complexities with which the President had burdened him.

Alice took her father's arm as they headed toward the main saloon to meet President Wedik. The Greens followed, both feeling the pulse of the sea under their feet. Despite their current troubles, Harcourt Green thought back to the time when they sailed together in a little thirteen-foot, one-sailed boat when they were just married. They had sailed, picnicked, made love, and talked endlessly. How long ago was that? He refused to count the years.

"Green, good to see you. Glad you came." Stanley Wedik opened the door to admit them into the saloon and played the host. "Come have a drink. Happy hour."

"Thank you, Mr. President. You know my wife, Frances. And my aide, Alice Ritter."

"Glad to meet you again, Mrs. Green. I'll just call you Frances, is that all right?" No reply was expected. Wedik continued with his greetings. "And this is the clever girl who made it through Annapolis. Affirmative action—it got you into a man's career didn't it, little lady? Great, I believe in giving the underprivileged a helping hand. Glad you're here."

John Ritter signaled his daughter by squeezing her arm tight enough to hurt. She managed to accept the President's greeting with a measure of self-control. Frances volunteered, "Yes, please call me Frances; but you surely don't want me to call you Stanley?"

"Sure, sure, we're shipmates, aren't we? Isn't that right, John? Shipmates just like you and Harry were."

"We were shipmates a long time, Mr. President," Ritter responded.

"Well, here's my shipmate, Mildred. She's my mate and we're on a ship so she's my shipmate. Right?"

"So she is, Mr. President." Green bowed to the First Lady. Mildred Wedik was getting more uncomfortable by the minute. She had often seen her husband with a few drinks, but here he was making a fool of himself in front of these two women. She gave each of them a long look. One was a ritzy bitch with money that made her think she had a monopoly on class. The other was a black girl who didn't say much but was thinking plenty.

There was no stopping the President now. Leaving Mildred Wedik's side, he stepped forward to take Alice Ritter's arm. "I'll bet you had a ball at the naval academy, Alice. All those young midshipmen. A girl like you would never be at a loss for company, eh?"

Alice tried to remember that this was her commander in chief. Green intervened hastily. "Lieutenant Ritter has been helping me in planning a response to the economic crisis. If it weren't for her, I wouldn't be as far along as I am."

"Harry, are you into an economic study?" Frances asked, making conversation.

Green felt chagrined at having let his assignment slip. He had never done that, even to Frances, in all the years of service. "Dammit, Frances, why couldn't you let it lie?" That was what he felt like saying.

Befuddled as Wedik was, he had the cunning to infer what Green was thinking. "There's no harm in you knowing, Frances. Harry is working for me in sorting out the conflicting advice that I have been getting on how to meet the inflation, unemployment, and balance-of-payments problem the country faces. It's not really a secret; we just don't want the press getting wind of the fact that Harry is doing the legwork for me. It would put too much pressure on him. Wouldn't it, Harry, eh?"

"It certainly would, Mr. President."

"Suppose we let the new arrivals get comfortable, Mr. President," John Ritter suggested. "The chief steward has promised us a great dinner. You'll have time to talk then."

"Sounds good, John," the President agreed. "I need a nap. I feel a little tired." Waving his arm rather unsteadily, he called out, "Coming, Mildred, old shipmate?" He reached for her hand but missed and had to support himself against the bulkhead.

Mildred Wedik led her husband to their suite. She hated mothering a drunken husband, even if he was President of the United States. That's what she had become, she thought, a mother to a born loser who somehow had fallen into a job he couldn't fill. She wouldn't let on, though. She was certainly not going to let that Frances Green lord it over her. "What does she know about economics and national crisis that I don't know? Nothing, but at least she has a man for a husband. She can't keep him, I bet. If it's not that black girl, it's somebody else he's got on a string."

The pair finally reached their suite. Wedik was very unsteady. He fell forward on the bed, and in an instant was in a drunken sleep.

Mildred Wedik sat watching through the glass as the ship got under way and headed out to sea. Some of the spray from the bow flew past her porthole as the vibration and roll increased. There were some clouds on the horizon, and the sea was becoming a little choppier. Mildred hated the ocean. It made her sick, and seasick pills made her feel sluggish. She didn't want to take anything that would slow her down in front of the others.

Meanwhile, the Greens walked arm-in-arm to their stateroom. The door had barely closed behind them when Frances Green wrenched herself free from her husband. She confronted him in a raging fury.

"Where were you last night?"

The admiral tried to place a conciliatory hand on her shoulder only to have her brush him off. "Please don't raise your voice, Frances," he urged. "The others will hear. I phoned the house last night and got the maid."

"You must have been relieved that I didn't answer the phone!"

"Yes, I was!" Green was becoming angry in spite of himself. "I can't talk to you anymore! Anyway, I told her to tell you I was tied up at the office."

"Where did you call from?"

"The office, of course. The maid must have told you that. Where else would I call from?"

"An apartment in Georgetown!"

A dark suspicion crossed Green's mind. "You don't mean . . ."

"Yes, I do! I followed you! I saw you go in!"

Green lost his temper. "You're a sneak, Frances!"

"And you're a liar! Will you give up your Georgetown baggage?"

"No! She's my escape from you!"

They glared at one another, exhausted by the fury of the

exchange. The sound of footsteps passing their door prevented them from resuming the quarrel.

"We've got to put a good face on it," the admiral muttered, "as long as we're aboard ship. Don't throw away your self-respect by making a scene."

Frances made a cutting retort. "At least I've got some self-respect left, which is more than I can say for you!"

She went to the bathroom and he heard the shower go on.

A couple of doors down the passageway, John Ritter was engaged in a confidential conversation with his daughter.

"Those apartment houses I invested in with Harry Green," the chief was saying, "are in a bad way. The red ink is splashing all over the place. With this recession, some tenants have moved to cheaper places. I wish I'd never let him talk me into it."

"Is there no way out?" Alice asked.

"Sure. Get a lot of money in a hurry. How to do it is the problem. We're running out our credit string and we have to make those mortgage payments. After the refinancing, they're higher than ever. If something doesn't happen soon, we could lose the buildings. And everything we've put into them."

"What could happen?"

"Well, Admiral Green could drop dead, and the business insurance would pay off the mortgage before the balloon payment is due."

"That's a terrible thing to say! You don't really mean it?"

Ritter caught himself. "No use going into those problems now, Alice, not aboard ship. And don't let on that I've said anything to you. We both know Harry's got a national problem on his hands. We don't want to make it tougher for him. Keep it under your hat."

Alice shrugged. "He's also got a personal problem."

"That van Thuys woman? Is she still around?"

"Very much so. And I'm sure Frances knows about her. It shows every time she looks at him."

"Well, let's forget all that for now. I'll try to run a happy ship on this voyage."

The chief left for the bridge, and Alice got ready for dinner.

The Wediks were first into the dining room. They stood at the doorway greeting their guests as they arrived. The President looked for all the world as if he had not touched a drop all day. Smiling, he stood aside to allow the others to precede him to the table, which was set for six.

"Who's driving the boat, Chief?" Wedik inquired after they sat down.

Ritter gave him a bland look. "The first mate is the ship's officer of the deck, Mr. President. He will call me if he needs me."

"You have an admiral here, too, if you need help, John. And your lovely daughter. Can she really run this boat, Chief?"

Green answered the question. "Alice Ritter is an officer in the United States Navy, Mr. President————"

The President interrupted, "Just kidding, Harry. A joke."

"Yes, sir. I guess I have lost my sense of humor these last few days."

"Sure, I was pretty uptight, too, until you volunteered to take this responsibility. Try to relax for now. You'll feel better when you get back on the job."

The stewards began serving amid light chatter around the table.

The ship shuddered slightly as it momentarily nosed down into a trough in the roughening sea. The glittering crystal on the table tinkled. Wedik looked apprehensively at the others, who seemed completely unconcerned. On the bridge, the officer of the deck watched the developing squall line on the radar. The weather service had predicted only a minor disturbance. John Ritter was ready to take charge of the ship in the event of any substantial change in the forecast. This bit of rain that might be coming up was, the officer of the deck decided, no reason to call him away from his meal.

Voluble in most circumstances, Stanley Wedik took food seriously. He plunged into the first course, leaving the First Lady to keep the conversation going.

"Admiral Green, I hear from Mr. Ritter that you are old friends."

"Yes, ma'am." Usually adept, Green struggled to make conversation. "We were in the service together when I was a young officer. There were some good times and some bad times, too."

There was a pause.

"Tell me about the good times, Admiral," the First Lady coaxed. "Did you have a girl in every port?"

"Not that he told me about," Frances volunteered.

Whatever Green might have said was interrupted by a loud crash. Dishes flew across the table. Glasses and silverware fell to the deck. The ship had nosed down in the trough of a deep wave. Slowly—so slowly it seemed forever—the *Chesapeake* raised itself on the next crest and there was a clattering of tableware once more.

John Ritter was on his feet headed for the bridge. He did not run, but he lost no time.

"We hit something!" Wedik shouted. "I felt it. This goddamn tub is going to sink!"

"Mr. President, sir," Alice said, "nothing of the sort has happened. That was just the trough of a deep wave. The ship is going fine."

The former cruiser nosed down deep into the swell of the ocean and then rose again. The stewards hurriedly cleared the table and secured the movable furniture to keep it from sliding across the room. With each hurried precaution, Wedik became more alarmed.

"This goddamn ship has hit a rock! I felt it! It's going to break up and we're all going to drown!"

Green started to protest, "Mr. President, really, this is just———"

"Are we going to drown, Admiral? Tell me the truth," Mildred Wedik quavered, pulling her chair next to her husband and clutching his arm.

"Of course not, Mrs. Wedik. We've merely hit some rough water—a squall. It's probably only a few miles across the weather front. Really, don't worry. John Ritter is an excellent master of this ship. He'll take us through."

"What is he going to do, Harry?" Frances asked. "Will he try to drive through the squall line or turn back?"

"That's up to John Ritter, Frances. He's the captain."

Wedik's voice rose to a new pitch. "Do you mean you're going to put our lives in the hands of that man? He's not even a real officer."

Alice was plainly offended and unwilling to hide it. "Mr. President, my father is a civilian now. But he was a chief warrant officer for many years. This is a situation he has faced many times. These storms often seem much worse than they are."

"How do you know that, missy?" Wedik exploded. "Where did you get all your experience? You're just another black girl who got into Annapo————"

Mrs. Wedik quickly interrupted him before he could finish the sentence. "Stop it, Stanley! Lieutenant Ritter is an officer in the U. S. Navy. You are her commander in chief. You owe her respect for her rank in our armed forces."

For once, Wedik looked abashed. "Mildred, you're right. Lieutenant Ritter, I apologize. I didn't mean what I said." Then the old Wedik reappeared. "But something has got to be done about this ship. Green, do something."

"Well, Mr. President," Green replied, "it's John Ritter's ship, and he has a right—a duty—to give the orders. But I'll go up on the bridge and check for you on what he's doing."

Green left the table. Alice went with him. The others fell silent. Wedik looked queasy.

John Ritter was on the bridge directing the helmsman. The weather was foul. The leaden sky matched the color of the sea so exactly that it was impossible to distinguish the horizon. The ship pitched and rolled as it cut through the waves. With each dip of the bow, salt water sprayed across the foredeck and ran off the side of the ship in streams. Smash in the trough. Up riding on the crest. Smash down again. Wind and waves, merged air and water. Ritter gave a quiet command to the helmsman, and the *Chesapeake* adjusted its course.

The ship plunged into a trough, and then rose again, bow

streaming boiling salt water. Green knew that the Wediks would be sick. He thought of going below to reassure them, and then thought better of it. Let them stew in their own juice—literally, maybe, he thought to himself. Anyway, Frances was with them. She would steady them down.

The *Chesapeake* plunged on into the storm. The horizon seemed even blacker than before. Ritter made no move to change course. "We're okay," he said.

"Thanks to you," Green said. "You know, it seems to me that the economy is like a big ship riding out a storm."

"In what way, Harry?"

"Well, in the normal course of events, the ship works in a self-correcting way. After all, the ship floats as a result of equilibrium. The buoyancy of the vessel cancels out the force of gravity tending to pull it to the bottom. Even when we get hit by high seas that scare the pants off landlubbers, we know very well that the ship will come up out of the troughs and ride out the next rise."

"Sure—provided the sea isn't so bad as to swamp us. In the long run, the pounding sea can break the back of a ship. You know that."

"Right, of course, Chief. But I was speaking of the normal course of events. This storm, for instance, is not the sort that will threaten the *Chesapeake.* "

They felt the wind shift along with the direction of the seas. The *Chesapeake* almost turned sideways in the trough. Ritter snapped commands to the helm and the ship came about.

"Too bad the ocean's in a bad temper," Green continued. "But you see, that's just it. You can't always count on the normal events that permit natural self-correcting factors. If you hadn't reacted just now, we would have been in trouble, even if this isn't a typhoon."

"But you can overcorrect too," Alice interrupted.

"Exactly. If the master is constantly shifting course at every blow, he's as likely to get the ship into trouble as get it out."

Ritter agreed. "The ship can't take the pounding of constant shifts and twists against the sea."

"Yes, but more than that. Suppose you reacted as you did just now, shifting course to head into the sea. But then suppose the sea shifted again. You would have put us even more broadside into the trough than if you had done nothing. The point is, you knew what to expect, and what the lags were, and reacted promptly. What I'm saying is that if the sea is bad enough—and the shifts are rapid compared to the lags in human reaction and the reaction of the ship—then shifting course might be the wrong policy. Ships do founder, even with the best of captains."

"Just as often, they founder because captains are too paralyzed to act."

"Sure, Chief. But I'm thinking of the dynamics of the system made up of the sea, the ship, and the captain."

"Nevertheless," Alice interrupted, "you have to be convinced that the natural forces will see you through the storm, and that the ship can take the twists and turns of the sea. If that's not true, then holding the steady course may be an invitation to disaster."

"All right, Harry," Chief Ritter asked, "how does all this sailors' talk tie in with the economy?"

"Well, there's a rough analogy. Of course, economics is not like seamanship. The economists don't agree as we just did. But I'm sure the economy is taking too much of a pounding. It's broadside to the waves of current events, and I can't be certain what commands to give to bring it around so it will ride out the storm. How do we steer our ship over the crest of inflation and out of the trough of unemployment? That's the question in a nutshell."

"You're the officer of the deck on the economic ship." Alice extended the analogy between economics and seamanship.

"I guess that's right. And the trouble is, the captain—the President—is leaving the command to me. Are the shocks we're facing the result of natural forces of an inherently unstable economy like a storm at sea? Or are they created by the over-steering government policy that reacts with lags, or with insufficient information that sets up disastrous fluctuations in what would otherwise be fairly smooth sailing? I could steer better if I knew for sure."

"Well, Harry," Ritter declared, "the officer of the deck has to do something when the captain of the ship is incapacitated. And in this case, you do have something to go on. What about Curtin's policies for fighting inflation?"

"There you have a classic case of oversteering. By the time he got elected and got around to contracting the money supply by appointing Christopherson to the Fed, the economy had begun to contract on its own. So his contraction plunged us into a depression."

"And then Wedik came in and reversed the policy of his predecessor?"

"That's right, Chief. Not only did he twist the Fed's arm to increase the money supply, but he was seen as ready to do so even more in the future."

"And so you think there were signals sent out that control of the money supply was going to be given up again. Oversteer in the opposite direction."

"Right, John, and so the cycle of peak and trough got even worse."

Alice put in a thought of her own. "Admiral Green, you've shown us an example of how it all might have happened. But that doesn't mean it's only the oversteering of the government that causes the waves. Maybe the ocean itself is causing them."

"That's true, Alice. And that's where I'm stuck." Green became thoughtful and then added, "My present problem in economics is not as personal as when I was with the naval procurement office in Norfolk a couple years ago. That was a small operation, where everybody knew everybody else. Now that I'm dealing with national problems, I have to rely on people I've barely met. In Norfolk, one enterprise did not affect the entire economic climate. But in the nation's business, each enterprise affects the rest, and the actions and reactions have a meaning beyond themselves. The whole is different than the sum of its parts. The Keynesians say the rules of the game are altogether different."

Suddenly the sky brightened even though the hour was well past midnight. The *Chesapeake* had broken through the squall line and was now in calmer waters. Through the breaks in the clouds the moon illuminated the still-churning seas and reflected back into the bridge. The bow of the ship sliced like a knife through diminishing waves.

"We had better go below, John," the admiral suggested, "and see how the President and the others are faring. I imagine you have to play host and I had better play the diplomat."

Ritter turned to his daughter. "Alice, will you stay on the bridge just a while longer?"

The two men departed, leaving Lieutenant Ritter to consult with the officer of the deck if trouble developed.

They found the President in better shape than when they last saw him. The calm sea had restored his self-control. He and Mrs. Wedik were watching a late-night talk show on television. Frances sat with them, bored and resentful, looking like a baby-sitter whose charges had worn her out and whose forebearance was exhausted.

"That was a short run through the squall," said Green. "Lucky for us it wasn't a long-run typhoon." The import of his words struck him as he finished speaking. He grinned and added, "In the long run we're all dead, Mr. President."

"What do you suppose he meant by that?" Wedik wondered, turning back to the television as the admiral left.

11

Assassination of an Admiral

Early the following morning, the Wediks, the Greens and the Ritters congregated on the deck near the helicopter. Admiral Green was as edgy as an ensign taking charge of his first sea party. He had to get ashore quickly and make one last rigorous effort to bring the economic factors into focus. He felt encouraged to find that the President was both sober and eager for him to fly directly from the ship to the White House. Frances Green and Alice Ritter would go with him.

"I'll follow when this ship docks," Wedik said. "Harry, I'm depending on you."

"Mr. President, I'll have a firm decision for you tomorrow afternoon. That's a promise."

The two men discussed the cabinet meeting on Sunday while the helicopter pilot started up. Mildred Wedik and Frances Green began to talk about shopping in Washington.

John Ritter tugged Alice by the sleeve, and they moved unobtrusively over to the rail out of earshot. "Alice, I can't wait on the apartment deal," he warned her. "I'll have to confront Harry Green before he ruins both of us. We might go under if he doesn't find more money for the mortgage payments."

"Are you sure it will be both of you?" his daughter asked in an undertone. "Are you sure he hasn't got a scheme to save himself and let you take the rap?"

Ritter frowned suspiciously. "I hadn't thought of that. You're way ahead of me, Alice."

"You're too trusting. I haven't been around Washington very long, but I've learned you can't be like that and hope to survive in this town. Not with anybody. I'll help you with Admiral Green when the crunch comes. I know something that will put pressure on him. After all, blood is thicker than water, Dad."

She broke off as Green called her over, "Okay, Alice. Let's go."

Minutes later they were airborne. Sitting between the two women, Green said a few words to his wife, who looked determinedly the other way. He turned to Alice, only to find his aide unaccountably taciturn. He retreated into his own thoughts for the rest of the flight. The chopper landed on the White House lawn. Frances refused his hand, stepped down by herself, and stalked off. Green shrugged philosophically, asked Alice to drive his wife home, and went straight to his office.

He took the typed notes on the economy and went through them line-by-line, marking essential points in red ink and adding notes in the margins. The pages, which covered his exchanges with Sokolow and Christopherson, contained excerpts Green had selected as good thumbnail summaries of the basic issues between the two.

Finishing the last paragraph, Green shuffled the pages together, laid them on the desk, leaned forward in his chair, and rested his chin on his clasped hands. Most of the pattern was falling into place in his mind, but a few points about the Keynesian position remained to be clarified. He already knew how Sokolow interpreted Keynes, but he felt he needed another voice. He suddenly remembered Howard Tilson. He dialed Tilson's number. "I'd like to pick your brain, if you don't mind," Green said. "By the way, this is being taped. Okay?"

"Go ahead, Admiral. I hope you turn out to be my kind of Keynesian. That's what the American people need in the White House."

"Come on, Tilson, are there as many kinds of Keynesians as there are supply-and-demand economists?"

"Well, you might call us post-Keynesians, but we represent what Keynes really meant, not what others have put on him."

Green groaned inwardly but spoke into the telephone. "Anyway, let me try a quotation from Sokolow on you. Here's what he said to me as I recall it. Quote: 'Macroeconomic management of effective demand to maintain full employment without inflation is an engineering problem in economics. In fact, some years ago an economist—half in jest—did a hydraulic model of the economy. He had colored liquids being piped around glass tubing labeled income, consumption, savings, and the like.' Unquote. What do you think of that?"

Tilson snorted at this echo of lectures he had heard during his student years. "Typical Sokolow exaggerations! Anybody reading that would think we can go from one steady-state situation to another. Keynes never said that. Sokolow is jamming what Keynes did say into an equilibrium mold, and misleading other economists into thinking there's a cut-and-dried engineering solution to our problems."

"It seems that way from Sokolow's description."

"*Seems* is right. Sokolow's talking about the flow of money. But to relate money flow to output, it's necessary to know what determines the price level of goods and services so that if you control the expenditures in money terms, you also control the output and employment."

"Doesn't the supply of money determine the price level?" Green asked.

"No, that's the monetarist view. Keynes showed that output is determined by aggregate demand for goods and services making up the national income. To get from money expenditures to the elements of demand in national income————"

"Consumption, investment, government, and net exports?" Green queried.

"That's right," Tilson said. "To translate those money demand flows into goods and employment in his hydraulic engineering system, Sokolow needs a way to fix prices. Following Keynes, he believes in prices being set by money wages, which in turn are given by what the workers take to be the going normal money wage."

"That seems silly to me," Green replied. "Aren't workers

concerned with what money will really buy rather than simply the amount of cash they receive in their pay each week?"

"Well, it is silly. Maybe it's convenient for Sokolow's version of Keynes, but it's more than I can take to believe that workers really suffer from money illusion as old-fashioned Keynesians like Sokolow believe. What makes him think workers are so dumb they don't realize that real wages, not money wages, are the important thing? Isn't it just upper-class snobbery to think that everybody else computes the real flow of goods and services they get, that only the workers are victims of money illusion and that they think only of the money they get rather than what they can buy with their wages?"

"Correct me if I'm wrong," Green said, "but wasn't that just Keynes's way of saying that wages are embodied in custom and union contracts, and therefore are difficult to reduce? Moreover, I have a hunch that Keynes knew it was politically impossible to try to get over the Great Depression by asking workers to be the first to reduce their income."

"Well, if you put it that way, Admiral, I agree with you. But then you're no longer talking about a true economic equilibrium situation, but rather a short-run stickiness in wages. You're talking about political situations in a period of turmoil."

Tilson shifted to the question of investment. "Keynes was describing a disequilibrium situation. Investment, by its very nature, denies equilibrium. It's an addition to the stock of capital equipment. It's extra capital, and hence tells us that the economy is not in a position of rest."

"What is this question really about, Tilson? Are you and Sokolow only discussing economic theory, or are there practical consequences?"

"Admiral, my old professor, Murray Sokolow, in talking about equilibrium, is misleading us. He wants us to believe that we can fine-tune the national interest when in fact we can expect only short-term relief from his program. It still is better than those reactionary monetarists and voodoo supply-siders, but it's only a short-term Band-Aid."

"In the long run we are all dead, he says," Green added.

"Sure, but there is another aspect to all his talk about the money illusion. Sokolow's reading of Keynes puts the burden of stopping inflation on labor. You see, he says that during the Depression wages could not be cut because workers had this illusion. Then he tells us that this was not a true case of near-sightedness, but just a short-run institutional effect of the Depression, which maybe was just a political reality. Now that we are fighting inflation as well as unemployment, he is all set to say that the illusion broke down because of the very success of the Keynesian program of full employment, so we have to clamp down on workers and unions. For all his liberal talk, Sokolow is working himself up to union busting! But really, wage increases are only one kind of cost-push inflation. Oil prices would be another example."

Green thought about the way in which turmoil in the Middle East had caused oil prices to rise and push up the cost of everything else.

Tilson kept talking. "There are two sorts of inflation—cost-push and demand-pull—that have to be considered. Aside from the unions' cost-push elements, a demand-pull inflation can occur if the government spends excessively during a period of nearly full employment. That includes entitlement programs to meet social needs, and large military expenditures that may be justified by the international situation."

"How might the expenditures be financed?"

"Most easily if the government borrows money from the banks," Tilson said. "Here the government enlarges the debt it owes the banks, and the banks, backed up by the Federal Reserve, create new money to lend to the government."

"So then an increase in debt is inflationary?" Green asked.

"Not necessarily. There are big only ifs: only if it occurs under conditions of full employment; only if the debt is sold to banks that provide new money with the aid of the Fed; only if the new money is actually spent by the government. That is to say, it's not the amount of debt or money as such, but whether it increases total demand above full-employment capacity. Then it operates as an 'inflationary gap,' just as inadequate demand is a 'deflationary gap' leading to unemployment."

"Then borrowing from the public is like a tax on the public, which it voluntarily accepts when offered enough interest. Is that right?"

"Yes. Borrowing entices funds from the public, while taxation takes them away by force of law."

"Now, finally, tell me about unemployment situations," Green suggested.

Tilson launched into that phase of the discussion. "When there is unemployment, neither taxation nor borrowing from the public makes much sense because what government spends on factors of production, the private sector does not spend. Actually there's a 'balanced-budget multiplier theorem,' which shows there is some limited increase in demand, even if government spending is totally financed by taxation. You see, you write an equation—but I won't go into that just now. Under conditions of unemployment, then, the effect of the increase in debt is to put people and resources back to work. There is no diversion of resources from private purposes and there is no inflation."

"You mean that the deflationary gap is reduced by government expenditures financed by borrowing?" Green queried.

"Exactly."

"And by tax reductions, too?"

"Sure, that's what John F. Kennedy did."

The remark made Green recall Tilson and Anderson quarreling at Frances's party over this same question. The recollection did not please him. The admiral glanced at his watch. Concluding that Tilson had nothing more to say that was new, Green brought the conversation to a close and went back to his notes.

He was deep in thought when Alice arrived in the office.

"I've deposited Mrs. Green at the house," his aide announced.

"How is she?"

"She seems mad about something."

"Did she say what it is?"

"No."

"Probably something I said last night on the boat."

"Could be." Alice's curt tone made Green look sharply at her. "Are you feeling all right, Alice?" he inquired.

"I'm fine, Admiral. Now I think I'd better get back to my desk if you don't need me here." Her face, usually so lively, was an impassive mask.

"No, you go ahead. There's nothing for you to do here."

As Alice vanished out the door, Green thought she might be feeling a delayed reaction to the voyage—especially to the President's gauche remarks. Well, she was level-headed enough to get over it. He went back to work.

He had much of his report finished in his personal cryptographic shorthand when the clock told him it was time to go home. Alice had already left.

When Green got home, the maid reported that Mrs. Green was upstairs in the bedroom. He went up and found the door locked. Knocking on the door and pleading with her to answer brought only a stony silence from inside. Chagrined, the admiral went downstairs and had dinner by himself. He slept in the guest room that night, rose at daybreak, and breakfasted alone. He drove to the White House mulling over what future lay ahead for him and Frances.

He arrived early at his office, where he spent some time studying his notes. Then he pushed them into a briefcase, left the White House, flagged a taxi, and told the driver to take him to the Pentagon. A few blocks away he changed his mind. He told the driver to take him to Marianne's apartment in Georgetown first, and to wait for him. After twenty minutes inside, Green returned to the taxi and continued on to the Pentagon.

Alice got to the White House office at her usual time. Surprised not to find the admiral there, she worked at some odds and ends for an hour. Then, concerned about where he could be, she decided to find him and make sure there was nothing wrong on this critical day.

She called Green's home first, let the signal sound a dozen

times, and gave up. "The Greens are both out," she thought. "I wonder if they're together."

On Green's desk she found a memorandum with a phone number and the name Professor Alan Claus. She tried the number. A man's voice answered.

"Professor Claus speaking."

Alice explained why she was calling him on Sunday morning.

"No, Admiral Green isn't here," Claus replied. "There's no reason why he should be. I'm just a professor of economics at Georgetown University. And I've already told him everything he wanted to know."

"Can you tell me what you talked about?"

"No reason why not. Monetary theory and econometrics. I'm a consultant to one of the new members of the Board of Governors of Federal Reserve System doing research on the theory and measurement of expectations. It's a new field—or at least I have a new approach to expectation formation. It has to do with how people react to inflation. The old monetarist theory was called adaptive expectation, which got all tangled up in problems of the long run and the short run. I'm concentrating on rational expectations to get a better theory."

"Well, if you're working for the Fed, I suppose that means monetary policy as well as theory."

"Very much so. I hope Admiral Green is taking what I said seriously. The market mechanism is the only way for this country. I have to go now. It was nice talking to you."

Alice sat thoughtfully for a minute or two, turning over in her mind the feasibility of doing what she felt she ought to do next. Time was running out. She dialed the number of Marianne van Thuys.

Marianne answered. Alice decided to skip the preliminaries. "This is Lieutenant Alice Ritter, Admiral Green's aide. Is Admiral Green there?"

Silence at the other end. Then, "I'm not sure I know what you mean."

"Ms. van Thuys, this is no time for games. Is Admiral Green there?"

In the background Alice heard a man's voice call, "Marianne, come back to the bedroom." Alice did not recognize the voice. But as faint as it was, she knew the speaker was not the admiral, who had an unmistakable gravelly voice. Suddenly the phone went dead, followed by a dial tone. Marianne clearly did not want to talk about Harcourt Green, if only because she was entertaining a different male visitor.

A few more calls proved fruitless. Alice fidgeted until the phone rang and she heard Green saying apologetically, "Alice, I'm sorry I forgot to leave a note telling you where I'd be this morning. I'm at the Pentagon working on my report. I'll phone you again in an hour or so. Meanwhile, get in touch with all the economists I've been consulting. They're liable to be upset about my not being at the White House if they try to phone me with last-minute advice. I've already talked to Frances."

"I'll take care of everything, sir," his aide assured him.

Alice listed the names of the four economists to be told Green's whereabouts. Sokolow and Christopherson both said they would be in their offices in case they should be summoned to the cabinet meeting. She tried Tilson's bachelor pad without getting any response. Claus was not at home. She left the message with his wife.

After that, Alice went to Green's desk and turned on his tape recorder. She listened to the admiral's conversation with Tilson and, since there was nothing else on the tape, turned the machine off.

She killed time until Green phoned again while she was looking at herself in the mirror. When they met at the Pentagon, he was pleased to find her back on an even keel with him after her recent exhibition of monosyllabic taciturnity. He guessed she had gotten over whatever had bothered her. They conversed in their old informal manner while driving toward the White House.

They crossed the Arlington Bridge, paused at the Lincoln Memorial, and continued up Bacon Drive until the red light stopped them in front of the National Academy of Sciences.

The admiral, in the midst of his remark about economics,

had no presentiment that a figure armed with a rifle was skulking behind the juniper bush on the academy grounds. The rifle pointed directly at the windshield on the passenger side of the front seat. A finger squeezed the trigger.

Harcourt Green never heard the shot that killed him.

At that moment, President Wedik and the members of his cabinet were assembled around a table in the White House. They all looked somber, feeling the tension in the room and the expectations outside across the country. The Secretary of State and the Secretary of the Treasury appeared especially uncomfortable. They would bear the main burden of defending the President's decision—Admiral Green's decision—whatever that might be, to critics abroad and at home.

Wedik tapped his fingernails on the table. "Maybe it's good Harry isn't an economist," he said. "He's been listening to both sides without bias. He's intelligent. He's been around. He's grasped the essentials by now, and he'll give us a reasonable presentation."

The Secretary of the Treasury checked his watch against the clock. "Mr. President, this meeting is due to start in twenty minutes," he commented.

"Harry's never late," Wedik replied. "He'll walk in the door any minute now."

A secretary appeared with a portable telephone. "For you, Mr. President. Urgent."

Wedik took the instrument. After a few words, his jaw fell and he turned visibly pale. His lips moved soundlessly before he managed to croak the words, "Send Lieutenant Ritter up at once!"

Replacing the phone with a trembling hand, the President looked around the circle of puzzled faces. "That was White House security," he told his cabinet. "Harry Green's been shot!"

A stunned silence fell over the room. "How bad is he?" the Secretary of the Treasury asked.

"He's dead!"

Pandemonium erupted in the room, a babble of incoherent voices that broke off as Alice Ritter came through the door escorted by a Secret Service agent. She was a startling sight in her blood-stained uniform. Her hair was disheveled, her eyes staring straight ahead.

The Secretary of State offered her a chair, and the cabinet officers at the table gathered around to hear her repeat the story of how Admiral Green had been assassinated while she was driving him to the White House.

Those present stated later that the tragedy seemed to bring out in Wedik an inner strength nobody realized he possessed. Rousing himself, he took command.

"We can't make a decision today," he said. "I'll order national mourning until after Green's funeral. That will give us a little time. After that, well, I'll just have to take the heat till we can formulate a policy. Unless," he added hopefully, "Harry wrote his report saying what advice he intended to give us."

"His briefcase is downstairs," Alice said. "I don't know what's in it."

"Get it," Wedik ordered an assistant. "Have you any idea who shot him?" he asked Alice.

"No, I didn't see the sniper. All I know is that the shot must have come from behind the juniper bush on the academy grounds."

"What's being done?" the President inquired of the Secret Service agent.

"Mr. President, the grounds of the academy are being searched right now."

"Let me know immediately if they find anything."

"Yes, sir." The agent left.

Green's briefcase was brought up. The typed pages told the group nothing more than what Murray Sokolow and Martin Christopherson advised. The rest of the contents were written in Green's cryptographic shorthand. No one, not even his aide, could make sense of the symbols.

"Admiral Green was like that," Alice informed the others.

"He wanted most of his secret notes to be unintelligible to anybody else. He used to say his system was unbreakable because he used only a few symbols in writing. The rest were in his head."

President Wedik's face betrayed his bitter disappointment. "We'll never know what was in Green's report," he lamented.

12
Who Is the Mystery Woman?

Two days later, Alice Ritter returned to Green's office in the White House. She hoped doing some work would help her regain her emotional stability. Being alone in her apartment made her prey to terrible memories and doleful reflections about her future now that the admiral was gone. She felt that she must do something to distract her from these thoughts, and cleaning up the office was the most obvious solution to her problem.

Alice found that all the classified documents had already been removed by officials at the White House. She therefore busied herself with the remaining files, correspondence, books, and magazines. They would have to be disposed of before another chief of staff to the President moved in. She began stacking things to be kept and dropping superfluous items into the shredder.

Every so often she paused to read a letter or flip through a publication. One glossy brochure caught her eye because it fell open to a page with a photo of Geraldine Anderson, the brilliant new economist at the Commerce Department. The profile gave a summary of Anderson's career, from her college days, through her campaigns for libertarian causes and her conservative political activities, to her work as an economist. This work included three years at the naval procurement office in Norfolk prior to her transfer to Washington.

Alice read the profile, put the brochure aside, and went on

with her cleaning up. She was so preoccupied that she jumped when the phone rang. Lifting the phone, she said, "Admiral Green's office" before she caught herself and broke off in confusion, remembering that Green was gone.

"I understand how you feel," said a sympathetic male voice. "I'm Jack Lebeau of the White House Secret Service. I saw you come in a little while ago. I'd like to speak to you."

"Is it about Admiral Green?"

"Yes."

"Come on up. I could bear to talk to somebody."

Lebeau arrived a couple minutes later. He was a black-haired, brown-eyed man of about thirty. Alice remembered him as one of the men who interrogated her just after the shooting. They exchanged pleasantries and condolences. Then the Secret Service agent drew a cassette from his pocket.

"I'd like you to listen to this and tell me what you think," he said.

"All right, go ahead." Alice gestured to the tape recorder on the desk.

Lebeau slipped the cassette into the machine and pressed the play button.

A man's voice said, "Is this the White House Secret Service?"

"Yes, it is," Lebeau's voice answered. "What can I do for you?"

"I have something to tell you about Admiral Green."

"Who are you?" Lebeau asked.

"I run a motel near Baltimore. I saw the stories about the Green murder. I thought it might help you to know that a couple of years ago, Green used to stop at my motel with a woman who was not his wife. The photos of Mrs. Green show she's a medium-sized blonde. I didn't see enough of the other woman to identify her, but I can tell you she was a tall brunette."

"Which motel is that?" Lebeau inquired.

"I'm not going to name it. I don't want to see any of this in the papers or on television. Green always signed in as Mr. and

Mrs. Well, that's all. You can take it from there. Don't bother tracing this call. I'm at a pay phone in Baltimore."

"One minute," Lebeau urged. "What about the car license? Can you tell me how Green wrote it in the register?"

"Sure, I have it right here." The voice gave the number, and then the phone went dead.

Lebeau turned off the tape recorder. "We've checked the license number. It's a phony. Well, Lieutenant, do you recognize the voice?"

Alice shook her head.

"Did you know about Green and the brunette at the time mentioned by this informant?"

"No, but that was before I became Admiral Green's aide," Alice pointed out. "I have no idea if they've been mixed up since I came aboard."

She and Lebeau discussed the problem for half an hour without making any headway.

"Looks like we're up against a stone wall with this one," Lebeau commented. "Well, thanks for your time, Lieutenant Ritter." He pocketed the cassette and left.

Alice leaned back in her chair, tapped a pencil against her chin, and said to herself, "So, there's a mystery woman in the case. I wonder who she is."

13

Suspects

Admiral Harcourt Green's funeral cortege wound its way through Washington to Arlington National Cemetery, where the deceased was to be buried. The casket was drawn on a flag-draped caisson, the slow march honor guard stepping to the sound of beating drums and muted brass.

A long line of cars followed the military procession. Frances Green, dressed in black, was among the first to reach the graveside. John Ritter supported her by the elbow, and Alice Ritter was on the other side. It was the first time they had seen her since her husband's murder. President Wedik and the First Lady walked from their limousine, escorted by Secret Service agents on the alert. Murray Sokolow and Martin Christopherson took their places in the group surrounding the grave, with Howard Tilson and Alan Claus nearby. Discreetly back on the fringe stood Marianne van Thuys.

The President himself gave the eulogy. He extolled his late chief of staff as a military hero. "He was," Wedik intoned in a baritone vibrato delivery, "the constant servant of his country in peace as well as war. He served in counsel as well as conflict. He struggled for national prosperity as well as national security. He admired Abraham Lincoln, as we all know. It is appropriate to quote the Great Emancipator on this occasion. It is altogether fitting and proper that we remember Harry Green on this hallowed ground . . ." The inflated rhetoric continued.

The final prayers for the dead were said by the presiding clergyman, the rites ended, and the crowd began drifting away.

"You have to say one thing for the President," Tilson remarked to Sokolow, "he knows how to run a first-class funeral."

Sokolow made no reply.

"The whole point about this dog-and-pony show," Tilson went on, "is to buy time. Wedik doesn't know what to do about the economic crisis, so he seized on this opportunity to shut the country down while he thinks of something. Harry Green never lived to tell Wedik what to do. But Harry Green in death is still of some use. I just hope Wedik has the sense to follow Keynesian policies, whether he understands the theory or not. We're the best————"

"This is no time to think about economics," Sokolow interrupted him. The chairman of the Council of Economic Advisers edged away and began to talk to the Secretary of the Treasury.

Frances Green drove home with John and Alice Ritter. They gathered in the sitting room and talked in the hushed tones of those just returning from graveside. This time communal mourning gave way to realism rather quickly.

"The authorities still don't know who shot Harry," Frances said. "The President told me so himself."

"Have you been interviewed by the FBI?" Alice asked.

"Not yet. I told them I wasn't up to it. You were, I'm sure."

"Yes, of course. I could only tell them the bare bones of what happened. I mentioned how I picked up the admiral at the Pentagon with the economic report he was working on. I told them the route we took, how we stopped at the Lincoln Memorial, and the last bit about the shot."

"What else?" her father asked.

"They asked me to describe what I did after the shooting, and why I didn't go to a hospital. I told them all of that. They asked if I saw the sniper. I told them no, but I thought the shot came from the juniper bush in front of the National Academy of Sciences building. I didn't see the muzzle flash of the shot, if there was one. I was looking at the red light."

"You got the hell out of there as fast as possible. Right thing to do," John Ritter said.

"Did they ask about the report that was in the car, Alice?" Frances inquired.

"I mentioned it, Frances. The President had a Secret Service agent bring it up."

"Do you know what was in the report?"

"No. I know the admiral had finished it and was ready to present it to the President and the cabinet. But he wrote his notes in his shorthand, which nobody could read. Not even me."

Her father placed his hand on hers. "Alice, have you any hard information on what position Harry finally took with respect to the alternatives facing the President?"

"No. He never told me. I've been thinking about it a lot, though."

Alice broke off at the sound of a car driving on the gravel. Whoever it was had been permitted past the security check established at the gates of the estate since the murder.

The doorbell rang. Frances Green opened the door to face a tall, muscular man in his late forties. "Mrs. Green, I'm Robert Brittain—two t's." The man smiled a little smile.

"Yes?"

"I'm with the Federal Bureau of Investigation." Brittain produced a wallet with an identification card from the breast pocket of his blue-striped suit. Frances could see the butt end of the pistol in his shoulder holster.

"You want to talk about the shooting," she surmised.

"Yes. Are you feeling well enough?"

"Yes. Come in."

"Thank you, ma'am."

Brittain followed Frances into the sitting room. "This is Mr. Brittain from the FBI to see me," she introduced him. "This is Lieutenant Ritter, my husband's aide, and her father, John Ritter."

Brittain extended his hand to the other man. "I have already met Miss Ritter. I appreciate your help with our investigation, Lieutenant."

"We'd better leave," Alice said.

"Stay to dinner," Frances asked. "We can have pot luck if you don't mind."

Alice accepted the invitation. "Sure, Frances. Dad and I will have a walk while you two are talking."

The FBI agent bowed politely as they left. He took an easy chair. "Now, Mrs. Green, maybe you can help us," he began the interview. "I know it's painful for you. But you surely want your husband's murderer brought to justice. Law enforcement authorities must gather all possible information before the trail grows cold."

"I'll help you all I can," she replied.

"When did you see your husband last?"

"On Saturday morning. We returned together from the *Chesapeake.*"

The agent raised his head from his notebook. "You didn't see Admiral Green between Saturday morning and the time of his death on Sunday afternoon?"

"No."

"Was he home Saturday night?"

"Yes."

"Was that unusual, Mrs. Green? I mean, that you didn't see him even though he was at home?"

Frances Green felt her temper rising. "I'm not going to answer that!" she snapped.

Brittain shifted his weight in the easy chair. "Could you explain that a bit? Admiral Green was not on active duty away from home."

"Really, Mr. Brittain, is this essential to your investigation? My husband was a very busy man; he frequently worked in his office long hours. He was working on a critical project for the President on the state of the economy that he had to get ready in time for the cabinet meeting."

"Yes, Mrs. Green, we know that."

"Well, that should tell you what he was up to. Shouldn't it?"

"That tells us what he was doing but not why he was shot or who shot him."

The detective extracted a small notebook from his overladen

breast pocket. He freshened the lead in an automatic pencil and resumed his inquiry. Frances Green nettled him. He wondered how the admiral had lived with this woman. She was not rude or really uncooperative. No, he couldn't say that, but she was goddamn superior. "Born with a silver spoon in her mouth, I'll bet," Brittain thought.

"What were the circumstances at your last meeting with your husband, ma'am?" he asked with studied politeness.

Frances explained that they had been on the *Chesapeake* with the President and some others. "The First Lady was there. Also John Ritter and Alice."

"Ritter? The gentleman who just left?"

"Yes, Mr. Brittain. He is captain of the *Chesapeake,* and in any case an old friend of Harcourt and me." Frances was irritated. Why did the interrogation require an explanation that the Ritters were also guests of the President?

"Well then, you were all aboard ship."

"Yes, Mr. Brittain. We were all at dinner when the ship ran into a storm. I suppose it was only a squall as Harcourt said, but it did kick up the sea quite a bit. Admiral Green and Lieutenant Ritter went up to the bridge with the captain."

"When did Admiral Green return to your cabin, Mrs. Green?"

Frances allowed no emotion to show. "He didn't."

"Why not?"

"Don't you think that is a bit personal, even for a G-man?"

Brittain made a conciliatory gesture. "Please forgive me. We do have to know all the details. I assure you, we are professionals—like doctors and lawyers. We have to deal in personal matters. It's all confidential. It might be easier for you to answer these questions here than in court—unless you felt it might incriminate you, and then you could———"

"What? Take the Fifth Amendment?"

"You don't have to testify against yourself."

"My God, are you accusing me of somehow being involved in the murder of my husband?" Frances was shouting now, her face beet red.

"No, no. Of course not. I'm sorry I upset you. These are only your rights. Please don't read anything more into what I said. But do tell me, if you would, what happened."

"We had a quarrel. It had been a difficult evening. The President was upset by the storm, and I was trying to help him and Mrs. Wedik. We had words and Harcourt spent the night elsewhere on the ship. I assumed he was on the bridge most of the time."

Brittain changed the subject. "Forgive me, Mrs. Green, but did it ever happen to your knowledge that Admiral Green was involved with other women?"

"How dare you ask that?" Frances was on her feet.

"I do have to know."

Frances glared at him. "You don't have to know from me! Why don't you read the gutter newspapers?"

"I'm sorry, Mrs. Green. I want to give you a chance to set the record straight, no matter how painful it might be."

Frances sat down again, struggling for self-control.

"Were there other women, Mrs. Green? Was that what you quarreled about?"

"Mr. Brittain, are you a married man?"

The investigator had not expected the question. "Y-Yes, ma'am," he stammered a little. "Yes, I am."

"Do you ever quarrel with your wife?"

"Look here, Mrs. Green, I am just doing my job in asking you these questions. I know it's difficult for you—even embarrassing—but I am the one who is asking and you are the one who is supposed to answer. Unless you refuse to answer, which is certainly your privilege."

"I am not refusing to answer your questions, young man. I only want you to remember that husbands and wives quarrel about many things. The things they mention may not actually be what's bothering them."

The detective sighed a patient sigh. "Mrs. Green, was the fact that your husband was unfaithful to you a part of your quarrel? Could you answer that directly, please?"

"Yes, it was a part but not all of it."

111

"What else was involved, could you say?"

"Over the years we had been growing apart. Communication had broken down, and so each of us didn't appreciate the good points or the accomplishments of the other . . ."

"Yes, Mrs. Green, I'm sure that's so. But the actual issue at stake was Admiral Green's involvement with other women, right?"

"With another woman, not women, Mr. Brittain."

"Then you know who it is he had been seeing?"

"Yes, I do. From time to time he visited a Marianne van Thuys. She's the daughter of one of the former Dutch engineers in Java. She lives in Georgetown."

"We'll have to consider her a suspect. This could be a crime of passion—perhaps a jealous rivalry. In any case, you knew about the liaison?"

"Yes."

"What did you do about it? Were you thinking of leaving him? A divorce even?"

"No, Mr. Brittain. I let life go on. I occupied myself with other activities. I loved Harry when I could. I hoped he would change. I hoped he would come back to me."

"Under the circumstances, you must have quarreled with him more than once," the G-man inferred. "Quarreled violently."

"That's a fair assumption," Frances admitted. "You might hear about it from my maid or somebody else, so I might as well tell you myself."

Again, Brittain changed the subject. "Did your husband have any enemies? I mean anyone who might have hated him enough to shoot him?"

"Not that I know of. Maybe there was somebody I didn't know about in his navy past. Maybe somebody who served under him years ago."

"We'll check that out, Mrs. Green. We still don't have a motive for the shooting. All we know is that it was very deliberately planned by someone who knew where Admiral Green would be. By the way, according to Alice Ritter, he phoned you from the Pentagon on Sunday morning. We know you were not at home after that. Our records show it."

"Are you saying I don't have an alibi?" she demanded furiously.

"Well, did anybody see you on Sunday?"

"No, I was at the Cathedral. And I didn't see anybody I know."

"Well, I'll list that as a coincidence."

"Dammit, man. Ask me! Did I kill my husband?"

"You asked it, Mrs. Green—not me. I'm not accusing you of anything at all. I do need to know where you were when your husband was shot."

"Well, sonny, you just take out your junior G-man mind-reading kit and find out. Get out of my house before I call a real policeman and have you thrown out!"

"Yes, ma'am. One more question. Can you shoot a rifle?"

"You know I can. It says so in that little notebook you're waving at me. It says right in my college transcript that I was captain of the women's sharpshooting team."

"All right then, Mrs. Green. Did you kill your husband?"

"No!"

"Did you arrange for someone else to shoot him?"

"No!"

"Do you know who did shoot Admiral Green?"

"No, but I wish I did."

"What would you do if you did know, Mrs. Green?"

"I would blow his brains out!"

"Thank you, Mrs. Green. That is all I need to know for the present. Have a good day."

The Ritters, walking on the grounds to kill time, saw the G-man drive away. They returned to the house and found Frances Green on the sofa sobbing. John Ritter helped her sit up while Alice poured a jigger of brandy. The bite of the liquor helped to calm her down. She described her encounter with the agent of the FBI.

"The authorities will want to talk to you again, Frances," Ritter pointed out. "And they'll talk to me too since I was Harry's partner in our real estate scheme. You and I had better have our signals straight on that one."

"John, is there something you're trying to tell me?"

Ritter nodded. "It's not as straightforward as you may think. We were in big trouble before Harry's death."

"Before?"

"Yes. Everything's changed now."

"How is that, John?"

Ritter fell silent, as if debating with himself how to put it. Alice intervened.

"Admiral Green talked to me about the reason for investing in those apartment houses. He said it was to take advantage of low interest rates. For a while, lenders underestimated inflation. For a while, interest rates were less than the rate of inflation that actually ocurred."

"That's the way Harry put it to me," Ritter took up the story. "He said that if we kept our money in the bank the real rate of interest after inflation might be zero or even negative. That's why he persuaded me not to keep much cash in the bank."

Frances Green nodded. "Harry never explained to me why you went into the real estate deal together. But I understand the economics of it."

"We put our money into buying the apartments instead of keeping it in the bank. We also borrowed a pile from the bank, in addition to the down payment, and bought the buildings in Dallas. It was a real gamble for me. After all, a navy chief's salary isn't that big. But I trusted him."

"I thought it worked out well, John."

"It did at first. We were able to write off the interest charges. The depreciation on the apartments was also deductible as business expenses on our income taxes, even though we borrowed the money to buy the buildings. The rent we were able to charge kept rising along with inflation. The mortgage payments we had to make remained the same through the years,

114

but with inflation they didn't amount to much anymore. We made money from inflation, especially when you consider the tax savings."

"What could have gone wrong, then?" Frances Green wondered.

Ritter squinted at her. "It's hard for me to say this, Frances, but Harry wasn't completely honest with me. After I read the partnership agreement and signed it, I figured that was that. After all, he was my friend. But just the other day I went back over the figures. Guess what I discovered? Harry was siphoning off some of our funds. He would have had to find more money somewhere to cover what he had taken and save our apartment deal."

Frances sat in stunned silence. She was not the bereaved widow any longer.

"John," she said at last.

"Yes, Frances."

"What sort of business arrangement did you have with Harry regarding those Dallas apartments?"

"What do you mean by 'arrangement,' Frances?"

"Well, were you organized as a corporation?"

"No, we were partners. Harry said there wasn't any sense going to the trouble and expense of getting a corporate charter."

"I see. What happens now that Harry is gone?"

"Legally, the partnership is terminated on the death of one of the partners. The assets of the firm have to be divided between the partners and their heirs. In this case, it's you and me."

"So we're partners? You and me?"

"No, not really. Harry and I took the precaution of taking out life insurance on each other for enough to pay off the outstanding loans and to buy out the other's heirs."

"You mean, Daddy," Alice interjected, "that if it had been you instead of Harry————"

Ritter finished. "Yes, you would have inherited my share and the admiral would have been able to buy you out. In that way, we could be sure that the business would continue without forced liquidation."

"Must I sell out my share to you, John?" Frances asked.

"That's what Harry and I agreed. His will specified that option for me. He showed it to me himself."

"He showed it to you? He didn't show it to me."

"Well, Frances, you know how things were . . ."

"Yes, I know how they were."

The three sat quietly.

Alice got up and walked to the footstool facing Frances. She looked deeply into the eyes of the older woman. Deep brown against pale blue. "Tell me, Frances, what you are driving at?"

"Well, Alice, your father is home dry, isn't he? He was up to his ears in debt on an apartment venture. Now he owns the whole show, including Harry's share!"

"Right on, Frances! Tell me about what I own!" Ritter was angry. "I went along with Harry and almost lost my shirt trusting him! I didn't have an admiral's pension! I didn't have a rich wife to bail me out!"

"Harry's death has saved you, hasn't it?"

The two were bickering now.

"Frances, go ahead and ask me whether I can use a rifle. Do I have marksman medals? Did I used to pick off floating mines with a bolt-action Springfield rifle?"

"All right, John, did you shoot Harry?"

"No. Did you, Frances?"

"No."

Alice rose and started pacing the room as she talked. "Face it, we are all suspects. I'm the only one with an alibi, and yet I could have set him up. I could have let the sniper know where the admiral would be on Sunday. The FBI will want to know who stood to gain if I did."

"If nothing else, your father's free and clear ownership of that Dallas property will come to you someday." Frances could not resist the temptation to bait her friend.

Alice replied in kind. "Sure it will. And you're relieved of an unfaithful husband." She checked herself, flushing with embarrassment. "I'm sorry I said that, Frances. I didn't mean it. You know that."

"Of course I do. Neither did I."

Ritter shrugged. "We'd better stop clawing at one another and try to help find the murderer. If we can."

Alice spoke up with abrupt loudness. "I have a confession."

14

The Murder Weapon

Orderliness was so ingrained in Robert Brittain's nature that he took it for granted. His desk was clear, his pencils sharpened and in a row, his calendar clearly marked with appointments for the month. How some of his colleagues at the FBI existed in a state of semi-chaos was a constant puzzle to him.

This feeling for the systematic and the methodical extended to his criminal investigations, where he believed that, given the goal of the felon, a clear pattern of rational, purposive action was usually present. That was the undoing of the criminal and the secret of Brittain's success as an investigator. Find the motive and then reconstruct the logical sequence of actions that the rational criminal would follow. Even a psychotic murderer could be rational in plotting orderly actions to meet an insane purpose.

Just now Brittain was seated at his desk in his office at FBI headquarters. He was talking to Salvatore Dannunzio, his assistant.

Dannunzio was short, with a shock of black curly hair that matched his eyes. Barely thirty, he was a contrast to the middle-aged senior FBI agent. Brittain was tall and blue-eyed. His straw-blond hair was beginning to turn gray at the temples. He combed his hair precisely over a thinning spot and looked a bit younger than his forty-nine years.

"So, you think the Green shooting was not a crime of passion? Is that it?" Dannunzio asked.

"No, Sal, you miss my point. This might well have been a murder by an injured wife, a spurned mistress, or a jealous rival. It could have been the result of a conspiracy of people with motivations ranging from cash to lust. That does not prevent whoever did it from being orderly, calculating, and deliberate in the assassination."

The younger agent shook his head. "That's true as far as it goes, Bob. There *is* often some underlying psychological rationality that leads in an unbroken chain from motive to act. Still, the means chosen sometimes tells you a lot about the murderer—or murderers—and the motives involved."

"How do we apply your idea to this case?"

"Well, look at the way Green was killed. First of all, take the weapon."

"U.S. rifle, caliber .30, 1903."

"Right, Bob, the Springfield rifle. That bolt-action piece was standard issue up to the Second World War, when it was replaced by the semi-automatic M-1, and then came the M-16 assault rifle in the Vietnam War."

"What conclusion do you draw from that, Sal?"

"It's an old weapon, but very steady, very reliable. Of course, anyone who can handle firearms could have used it, but it seems to me to point to someone with military experience. Someone who knew enough to choose it as the ideal sniper's weapon. He———"

"Or she."

"Or she did not choose to spray the car with bullets. The killer planned on a single shot, chose the weapon that would deliver the bullet very accurately, conceived a bold ambush that anticipated the route of the victim, and then hit the victim and nobody else."

"Like the driver," Brittain suggested.

"Like Alice Ritter," Dannunzio agreed.

"Sort of William Tell with a rifle. One shot hitting the bull's-eye."

"Sort of, Bob. Only the target wasn't an apple."

Brittain fell silent. He picked up the pencil on the right of the file arranged at the corner of his desk and began to draw little interlocking boxes on the note pad secured to the blotter on the right side of the desk.

"That's interesting," he commented. "Where would somebody get a World War One rifle, I wonder? I know there were some that were converted into hunting rifles. They were in use for a long time. The stocks were shortened and they were drilled for telescopic sights. That meant the bolts had to be bent to allow the sights to fit. All that."

"Well, the interesting thing," Dannunzio pursued his thought, "is that none of that was done to this weapon. Whoever used it was so sure of himself that he didn't use a telescopic sight."

"That might have been an advantage with a fast-moving target," Brittain cut in.

"Right, but more important, I think, is that using an old gun left no trail that would lead to a gunsmith who modified the rifle. The murderer used a weapon that did the job. Then he felt safe to abandon it in the bushes where we found it. He just walked away. There was no gun to conceal during the getaway. That would have been a real problem in broad daylight in Washington, D.C. Who knows when he brought the gun to the ambush site? But having used it, all he had to do was leave."

"He was lucky there were no bystanders or other cars on Bacon Drive or Constitution Avenue when he was drawing a bead on Admiral Green," Brittain pointed out.

"It was a carefully planned but very bold method of operation, wouldn't you say?" Dannunzio suggested.

"Yes, I would. Precise. Military."

"The kind of operation Green himself would have planned, if he had decided to commit murder."

"Well, I agree with you, Sal. The means could be the rational—or irrational—element that breaks the case. It tells us something about the murderer."

The men fell silent, absorbing the train of thought into their conceptions of the mind of the killer. Finally, Brittain spoke up. "I ask again: Where would anyone get a rifle used in the First World War?"

Dannunzio felt a degree of satisfaction that his superior should ask the question. "I looked into that. It seems the navy used the Springfield rifle all through the *Second* World War. Of course it was not a rapid-fire weapon; the bolt had to be operated manually after each shot to put another cartridge in the firing chamber. The army wanted firepower, but the navy needed accuracy and long range, along with simple maintenance. It needed a weapon that would be used only in special circumstances."

"Like what, Sal?"

"Like carrying ashore on the occasional landing. Or clearing floating mines."

"Clearing mines?"

"Yes. The minesweepers would extend devices that cut the cables holding floating mines just under the surface of the water. When they bobbed to the top, they were exploded by rifle fire. The marksman had to hit the tip of the horns projecting out of the mine in order to explode it. It took a great rifle to do that, and an expert shot, Bob."

"Who could have put their hands on the gun?"

"That's the trouble. Almost anybody could. At the end of the war, all weapons were supposed to be turned in. But in the great mad rush to discharge people from the service, that rule turned out to be a farce. All kinds of weapons and ammunition were removed from the naval discharge centers. Some were souvenirs, but there were lots of weapons simply taken home for use in hunting and whatnot."

"That's a dead end," Brittain surmised. "Those rifles have been lying unaccounted for in gun collections, hall closets, attics, and barns for over forty years. We have no way of telling who got possession of this gun, or where."

"It's a dead end if you mean that the murder weapon isolates the user and provides evidence that will hold up in court, Bob. However, it suggests things to me about the killer—or the killer's psychological makeup. You might not agree with my approach."

"No, you've convinced me, Sal. Let's play this out a bit further. I want you to make a list of all the people Green saw in the past two weeks. You can get that from Alice Ritter, his aide, and from his wife. Then let's see who was in the service. Let's look for navy connections especially."

"That's not necessary, Bob. I already did."

The older agent was irritated, but he tried to conceal his pique. "That's very good, Sal. Shows ambition. What did you find out?"

"Until the week before the shooting, Green's associates were the kind you would expect. Various government officials, military and diplomatic liaison, that sort of thing. Then, on the Thursday before he was murdered, he started meeting with the top economic officials, headed by Murray Sokolow of the Council of Economic Advisers and Martin Christopherson of the Federal Reserve System. Most of the time he was accompanied by Alice Ritter."

"She made out the schedule, knew where he would be?"

"Yes. She even knew some occasions when he went to see his mistress, that van Thuys woman. She volunteered the information. I didn't have to ask."

"Did you talk to Sokolow and Christopherson, too?"

"Yes sir, I did."

"Busy fellow, aren't you?"

Dannunzio ignored the barb. "I talked to Sokolow first. It seems he was in his office in the Old Executive Office Building at the time of the shooting."

"How do you know he's telling the truth?"

"I checked with the White House that he was to be on hand for consultations on Sunday."

"He's not a member of the cabinet," Brittain pointed out.

"No, he's an adviser to the President. He was standing by in his office in case he was needed, since the President and the cabinet were due to make an important economic policy decision."

"Anybody see him?"

"The security guard did. He remembers Sokolow coming in Sunday morning, but beyond that all he knows is that Sokolow left the building a few times to go to the White House. The White House logs show Sokolow came in three times."

"Christopherson?"

"Same thing. Except he was at the Fed building."

Brittain grimaced. "That means Christopherson was right next door to the scene of the crime. He might have spotted the shooting if he'd looked out the window."

"Not quite, Bob. You can't see Bacon Drive from his office. Anyway, the strange thing is that both Sokolow and Christopherson have backgrounds related to the navy. Sokolow was in the Marine Corps, and Christopherson was in one of those river patrol boats the navy had shooting at the Vietcong along the Mekong River."

"That's not so strange," Brittain corrected him. "Lots of civilians around Washington were in the service. Neither of them has a motive that I can see. People don't kill each other over economic theories."

Dannunzio shook his head. "That's not what Alice Ritter told me when I interviewed her. She was telling me about this hot dispute between Sokolow and Christopherson. They both were out to influence the President through Admiral Green. She thought they both were capable of anything to get their policies adopted. The country in mortal danger otherwise, and so on. She says they've been feuding about it. Really feuding."

"Sal, you'll believe anything if you believe that. They had nothing to gain except making their point. Sokolow is a former professor, isn't he? And Christopherson is a former banker. They're secure in their jobs, or if they're not, they can do better financially in the private sector. If they lose out in government, they can go elsewhere."

Dannunzio took a cassette from his pocket. "Before you go any further," he said, "here's something I'd like you to hear."

"What is it?"

"A tape of my talk with Alice Ritter. She knew I was taping her, but she spoke freely all the same. It's about economics. She wanted to tell me what she had heard from the two sides. She was pretty distraught at the time, and I think telling me all this was a crutch she could lean on. So I let her have her head. If I play snatches of our conversation, you'll get an idea of how serious she was, and why I took her seriously."

"Go ahead," Brittain invited. "Be my guest."

His subordinate slipped the cassette into a machine on the desk and pressed the play button. They heard Alice Ritter speaking. Her voice had a distinct quiver at the start.

"The Keynesians have an instinct left over from the Depression days. It's to increase government spending or to increase the money supply to stimulate private business borrowing for investment purposes."

"So these Keynesians are for increasing the money supply?" Dannunzio echoed her remarks to keep her talking.

"Well, not as an end in itself, although they're willing to do it as a means to their program. Depending on circumstances, they're for a mixture of tax cuts and government expenditure as long as there's unemployment. Their game is to drive down interest rates and, therefore, encourage firms to borrow and invest for business purposes. If that sort of monetary policy won't work, then they think government ought to spend directly."

"Keynesians are, therefore, always for increasing demand. Is that right, Alice?"

"Only if there's unemployment that can fairly be attributed to insufficient demand. But judging from the people I talked to, they interpret rather broadly the problems that can be dealt with by increasing demand. For instance, they argue that racial discrimination can be mitigated by increasing the demand for labor. It's true, you know, that we blacks are offered more jobs in a tight labor market."

Dannunzio made an embarrassed reply. "That's still one of the inequities of our system, Alice. I wish we could be as democratic in practice as we are in our Fourth of July speeches. But the point you're making . . . I suppose there could be too much demand even for Sokolow."

"Sure. Then he would be worrying about a 'demand-pull' inflation, rather than 'cost-push' inflation, and the appropriate medicine would be less spending by government and contraction in the money supply to raise interest rates. He says he would cut military spending because of its impact on the deficit.

He would bow to the inevitable and increase taxes to balance the federal budget and restrain inflation."

"I guess I see the picture now. Sokolow comes on like a Roosevelt-type liberal," Dannunzio inferred. "Unemployment is his main enemy, and he would be willing to put up with some inflation in order to reduce it. The only trouble is that we have not had a little inflation, but a lot of inflation. That makes it impossible for him to simply say go ahead and increase demand, even though it seems to him the only way to get a handle on unemployment."

"Yes, and as I said, to get at some of the problems that are solved by high levels of employment. I'm of two minds about this. As a black American, I would like to see a tight labor market where blacks can find jobs. As a naval officer, I favor government spending on the armed forces. Yet at the same time, I am afraid of the inflation that comes from too much demand."

Alice's voice was beginning to sound stronger. Dannunzio helped her along with another question.

"And what advice are we getting from Christopherson?"

"Well, even though he *is* a monetarist, he says there are things that monetary policy cannot cure."

"Like what?"

"Like unemployment, for instance. At least the sort of unemployment he would call the natural rate of unemployment."

"Well, where does it come from, according to the monetarists?"

"Partly from the structure of the labor market, and partly from the actions of government itself."

"How?"

"The structural aspect of it, they say, has nothing to do with total demand being high or low. Rather, it is a matter of workers being in the wrong place with the wrong skills. It also has to do with racial discrimination making people seem unable to fill certain jobs or discouraging them from getting the education and training to fill them."

"Well, surely that has to do with the level of demand. Sokolow certainly seems right there. When we had a tight labor market, as during the Second World War, then unemployment went down. Employers and unions even forgot about their racial prejudices in the rush to hire workers."

"Well, I can tell you that all the market-oriented economists don't go along with Sokolow's analysis," Alice said. "Their point is that the market forces of supply and demand will tend to wash out these structural elements in unemployment. People will find the right job skills and locations. Employers will abandon racial prejudices if they see that they don't pay—after all, they lose workers they might need."

"So where does the structural unemployment come from?"

Judging from her tone, Alice was getting back into her normal stride. "Well, market-oriented economists say it comes largely from government interference with the market. Just by managing total demand to get full employment, government prevents the market from pushing people to acquire the skills they need. Christopherson's point is that all the government social welfare programs that came in with Roosevelt and were expanded by Kennedy and Johnson turned out to be counterproductive."

"So the monetarists are not concerned with demand," Dannunzio said, "the way the Keynesians are?"

"It's not that they're unconcerned about it. In fact they catch flak from supply-side types who claim they pay too much attention to the demand side as influenced by the money supply. Christopherson feels it's something that should not be managed by the government, which will always make a mess of it. He feels that in the long run, left to its own devices, the supply-and-demand process will see to it that there's enough demand."

"It's a paradox, Alice. According to the monetarists, if the government intervenes, it will bring about the very conditions it's trying to overcome."

"That's right. You can see why Sokolow and Christopherson are at the point of open warfare."

Dannunzio seemed to be enjoying the lesson in economics. "I see what you mean. They both think they have to save the country from damned dangerous fools. The trouble is that each thinks the other is the fool!"

"That's the truth," Alice said. "We have two highly trained economists who at almost every point favor policies that are direct opposites of one another."

"Somebody is going to have to decide what to do."

Alice Ritter spoke dispiritedly. "That's what Admiral Green was supposed to do."

At that point, Brittain interrupted the tape. "I've got the gist of it, Sal."

"Listen to a little more further on," his assistant urged. "You'll hear Alice Ritter mention a pretty big number."

"Okay. Go ahead."

Dannunzio pressed the fast-forward button, made a few adjustments, and allowed Alice's voice to come through again.

"Gross National Product," she was saying, "is the name given by the U.S. Department of Commerce to the new value added by production in a given year. For example, in 1987 it was, wait a moment, let me look at my notes—yes, here it is—almost four and a half trillion dollars."

"You mean the United States produced four and a half, with twelve zeros after it, of goods and services? That's an awful lot of consumer goods and new machinery."

"Yes, but besides consumption and investment, that figure includes goods and services for the government. For instance, naval personnel are providing services to the country. And, of course, our ships and shore installations are bought by the government as well."

"Are you saying," Dannunzio responded, "that the navy is in the same category as people receiving government subsidies? Are naval personnel getting a handout like the airlines and the civilian maritime industry, or people on welfare?"

"No, the expenditures in your second group are transfer payments. The government transfers wealth from one group— say, taxpayers—to another for purposes other than the production of actual goods and services. There are transfer payments in private business, too. Sales of real estate, stocks, and bonds are very large, but they don't enter into the GNP because they don't represent new goods and services. They're transfers of previously existing wealth."

"How about foreign trade?" Dannunzio wondered.

"Our exports are part of the product of the United States. But since we would have to subtract the portion of consumption, investment, and government purchases that was used here but produced abroad to get the GNP of our country, the Commerce Department reports net exports as a component of the GNP. Net exports are exports minus imports."

"Well, if the GNP grew so much, that's great!"

"Not really," Alice replied. "You see, prices rose almost as fast as the GNP measured in current money prices, so the physical volume of production increased only slightly."

"If you say so, Alice."

"I do, Sal."

It was the first time she had used his name. He felt flattered. It showed in his voice.

"Inflation hurts everybody," he said.

"Actually, people can gain from inflation if they guess right," Alice corrected him. "My father didn't keep much money in the bank because he thought its value would fall."

"What did he do with it?" the FBI agent asked.

"He put his money into real estate. He bought some apartments in Dallas in partnership with Admiral Green. They borrowed a lot of money from the bank in addition to the down payment."

"Has it paid off?"

"Yes and no." Alice explained the real estate deal John Ritter and Harcourt Green had been in together. Then the tape came to an end.

Dannunzio turned the machine off. "What do you think, Bob?" he inquired.

"I think there are several motives for murder on that tape, Sal. First we have those fanatical economists. And then the Ritters. Which brings us back to the murder weapon."

"How so?"

"John Ritter was in the navy. Alice Ritter is a graduate of Annapolis. They both know how to use a rifle."

"But Alice was in the car when the shooting took place," Dannunzio protested.

"Sure. But she's been under fire in simulated battle exercises at the naval academy. I'd say she wouldn't flinch if a bullet passed that close to her. Not if she had faith in the sniper's marksmanship. And especially not if the sniper was her father. He gained a bundle as a result of Admiral Green's death. That will come to her when John Ritter's gone. She's a natural suspect, and so is he."

"Frances Green knows how to use a rifle. You came up with that piece of information yourself, Bob."

"So we can list Frances Green along with Sokolow, Christopherson, John Ritter, and Alice Ritter. And they're only the suspects we already know about. Looks like we have a lot of investigating to do, Sal."

15

Cry Bloody Murder

Frances Green and John Ritter stared at Alice, who appeared conscience stricken as she repeated her statement, "I have a confession."

"About what?" Frances asked.

Alice sat rigidly in her chair, her hands clasped in her lap, her fingers twisting convulsively.

"I've been providing navy intelligence with a log of Admiral Green's meetings with Marianne van Thuys. Whenever I knew he was seeing her, I informed my contact."

John Ritter gave a low whistle. "You'd better tell us about it, Alice."

"Yes, I want to," she replied. "Well, several months ago, shortly after Mr. Wedik took over as President, I had a visit from a Commander Donald Stock."

"Commander Stock? Commander Stock? I don't know of any Commander Stock in the navy. Did he have identification?"

Alice nodded. "He matched the photo on his ID. I had no reason to be suspicious of him when he said he was from navy intelligence. He said they were worried about Admiral Green's involvement with a mistress—a blonde foreigner named Marianne van Thuys. He said they weren't passing judgment on the admiral's private life, but they were concerned that a security problem might arise."

Frances Green spoke harshly. "Like what, Alice?"

Alice was apologetic. "I'm sorry, Frances. This Commander Stock—if that's really his name—said the admiral was getting so involved that he might be blackmailed. I told him Admiral Green would never breach security, but he insisted that intelligence was only taking precautions. He convinced me that I would be doing my duty as an officer in the U.S. Navy. And he promised me that everything would be done so discreetly that the fact would never be known outside navy intelligence unless Admiral Green proved to be a security risk. Since I knew that would never be the case, I decided I ought to go along."

"So you cooperated after that?"

"Yes, Frances. I'm sorry."

"That's all right, Alice. I can take it. But what did you do for navy intelligence?"

"Well, Commander Stock said they had installed a recording device in Marianne's apartment. It had to be very small, and it couldn't be simply a radio that sends signals to another location because that kind of transmission could be picked up from the outside by somebody else. They needed a recording device that could be turned on by a short signal sent as a pulse through the house current."

John Ritter saw the point. "With the device installed, all they needed to know was when Harry would be at the apartment so they could arrange to start the machine. And you were there to tell them. How did you do that?"

"I dialed a number and said simply 'Georgetown,' and they took it from there."

"Alice," said Frances, "dial that number now."

The lieutenant picked up the phone and pressed the buttons while the instrument sounded its seven tuneless notes. She listened and then held up the receiver for the others to hear. A woman's voice announced to all who cared to listen, "You have reached a number that is no longer in service. If you have dialed in error, please try again. This is a recording."

The trio sat stunned.

Then John Ritter said, "We'll have the police check with the phone company about that number. But I doubt if it will do any good. Whoever did it will have covered his tracks. But the method used must mean that Marianne van Thuys doesn't know about the bug in her apartment. It could still be there. Before we do anything, I'll find out if navy intelligence is really mixed up in this. I have an old friend over there from my time in the navy. He'll tell me."

Ritter made the call and then reported to the two women, "There's no Commander Donald Stock in the navy, and intelligence never kept Harry under surveillance."

"Then who handed me this story?" Alice asked.

"That's what we'll have to find out," her father replied.

Frances stirred in her chair. "If Marianne van Thuys doesn't know about that tape in her apartment, I think I should tell her. I want it destroyed. I can't bear the thought of anyone hearing what he said to her. It's too degrading."

Ritter looked doubtful. "What makes you think she'll destroy it?"

"She won't want her talk on the tape to get out either. Harry isn't here to be blackmailed, and a woman in her position can't afford to have her confidential conversations with her clients in the public domain. She wouldn't have any more top men in Washington calling her. No, she'll be willing to destroy the tape. I'm sure of that."

Frances rose and added emphatically, "I'm going to Georgetown! Will you come with me?"

Alice looked quizzically at her father.

"I don't think any of us should go," he said. "When you tell Marianne there's a bug in her apartment, she certainly won't destroy it just like that while you watch. She'll want to play it first and see what's on it. And she may refuse to talk to you, Frances. Have you thought of that? She may snub you. Besides, suppose somebody sees you. It might get out that the widow of Admiral Green has been calling on his mistress. Wouldn't that be a pretty scandal!"

Frances looked deflated. Her shoulders sagged. "Maybe you're right," she admitted. Then she straightened up. "But I can't sit around here any longer. My nerves are too jumpy. I'm going for a drive. Will you come with me?"

Again Alice looked at her father.

"Go ahead," he said. "The drive may do both of you good. I'll stay here and monitor the phone is case anything breaks."

The two women went out and got into Frances's red sports car. Frances drove. They went over and over the problem of what to do about Marianne van Thuys as they drove through the suburbs of Washington at random and then into the city. It was drizzling as they crossed the center of Washington. Almost before she realized it, Frances took them into Georgetown.

Her emotions boiled over into a sudden decision. "Alice, I'm going to the apartment. I'm going to see Marianne van Thuys and tell her plainly that she has a tape hidden somewhere in her rooms—a tape of great importance to both of us."

"But you don't know how she'll react," Alice protested.

"No, I don't, but I'll have to take the chance. I can't just let the tape stay there unknown to her. Suppose somebody should find it. Suppose the person who planted the bug comes back and gets it. My husband's intimate talk with his mistress might be played anywhere. I can't have that! She's got to know!"

The intensity with which Frances spoke made Alice realize the futility of trying to talk her out of it. It was plain that, her vanity threatened, the admiral's widow was not going to be stopped by cautionary advice. Alice remained silent as Frances drove to the apartment and drew to a halt at the curb.

"Alice, I know you don't approve of this," Frances said. "But you must see my point."

"Yes, I do, Frances. And I won't make any waves about it. I'll wait for you here."

Frances thanked her, got out, and walked across the sidewalk. She wondered if Marianne would answer her call at the front door, but the problem resolved itself because the front door was ajar. Frances found Marianne's name in the line of mailboxes and went up.

Light showed under the door to Marianne's apartment as Frances rang the bell.

No answer. She rang again. Still no answer.

Frances knocked and tried the door. It swung open—unlocked. The brilliance of the lights inside startled her after the glowering night. Frances entered the elegant apartment that

133

Harry had visited to find—what? Sex? Solace? Escape? The vaguest hint of spice hung in the air. Even though the fire was out in the brazier on the low table, the scent seemed to originate there.

Gingerly, Frances stepped further into the living room. She rested her hand on the sofa and called out to Marianne. "Are you there? Marianne van Thuys, are you home? I am Frances Green."

Silence continued except for the hiss of traffic outside as tires drove over wet pavement. Perhaps Marianne was out. Well, Frances could not wait. Her nerves were on edge. Now that she was here, the best thing was to find the bug and get away.

Where could a recorder be hidden? she wondered. Small. Accessible to electric current. Easy to recover, say, by someone claiming to be a maintenance worker. Where? There had to be at least two of them, Frances reasoned: one for the living room near the sofa, and . . . with a grimace, she guessed there would be one in the bedroom.

Frances picked up the telephone on the end table near the sofa. It rewarded her with a dial tone. She followed it to the wall connection. The telephone cord ended with a modular jack, one that simply snaps into place without the need of a telephone company installer. "Not likely," she thought. "Possible, but not likely. Where else?"

A little red reflection in the brass brazier caught her eye. Looking upward she saw the smoke detector. Its little red eye cheerfully told all that it was on watch. Frances stepped up on the table and, reaching up, unhinged the cover. She found it! "Beep!" the device reminded her of its original purpose.

"Now for the bedroom," Frances mumbled. The bedroom door was closed. She opened the door and in the darkness groped for the light switch as she entered. Frances stumbled over something soft and fell on it. Her face was against another face. Female. Cold. Inert lips parted in death.

Frances pushed against the body of Marianne van Thuys and scrambled to her feet. Horror and shock drained the blood from her face. She found the light switch and pushed it on—her bloody fingers leaving five trails on the wall leading to the switch. On the floor the sophisticated Continental beauty of Marianne van Thuys's face remained—undistorted even in violent death. Her chest had been torn open by the force of a large-caliber bullet that spattered blood over her nightclothes and negligee. Legs askew, torso contorted, face and body were a contrast in beauty and brutality.

Frances bent down and picked up a .45-caliber automatic from the floor. The sound of footsteps behind her made her whirl around in a panic, and the automatic went off over the head of a man rushing toward her. Robert Brittain wrenched it from her hand.

"I'll take the gun," he said grimly, "before you take another shot at me!"

"It just went off," Frances gasped. "It was an accident."

Salvatore Dannunzio appeared in the doorway holding Alice Ritter by the arm. Alice stared in horror at the crumpled figure on the floor.

"I found her—like this," Frances faltered.

Brittain bent over the corpse. "She hasn't been dead very long, Mrs. Green. Can you tell me what you are doing here?"

"We came to search . . ." Alice started.

"Please be quiet, Lieutenant," Brittain commanded. "Now, Mrs. Green, will you please explain yourself?" Weapon with the suspect's fingerprints, he was thinking. Literally, Frances Green had been caught redhanded. And Alice Ritter was her accomplice.

The two women were informed of their rights and taken to the district jail, where they were searched and fingerprinted. Common sense dictated that they refuse all statements until they had a chance to consult an attorney. Brittain demanded to know the purpose of their visit to the Georgetown apartment. Where had Frances gotten the gun? Was it her husband's? There was no point in cooperating with the FBI agent, she thought. His mind was already made up. Knowing that anything she might say could be held against her, Frances refused to answer any questions at all.

Interrogated separately, Alice insisted that she simply had driven with her friend to see the van Thuys woman. Brittain demanded to know the purpose of the visit. Alice stonewalled. "You will have to ask Mrs. Green."

"Did you volunteer to go with her?"

"No comment."

"Weren't you curious as to why she wanted to see the woman who was involved with her husband?"

"No comment."

"Why didn't you go in with her?"

"I want to make a phone call."

"That's your right."

Alice called her father and explained the situation. He assured her that he and a lawyer would be there shortly.

Brittain again sat facing her in the interrogation room. He took out his notebook, consulted it slowly, and faced Alice again.

"Alice . . ."

"Call me Lieutenant Ritter, please."

"Lieutenant Ritter, if you wish. I called you Alice because we ought to be friends. After all, we both are United States officers, aren't we?"

She gave him a stony look.

"Come on, Lieutenant Ritter. We're on the same team. Aren't we?"

"I am not involved in the murder of Marianne van Thuys and neither is Frances Green. So how are we on the same side when from the start you have been accusing us? First you suggested that she was involved in the assassination of her husband, and now you have your mind made up about this second murder. Haven't you?"

"Alice—Lieutenant Ritter—now you're the one being unfair. Surely you must see that the objective evidence does point toward Mrs. Green's involvement. Motive, opportunity, access, and skill with firearms."

"I have nothing to say to that."

"You don't have to. Of course you don't want to do anything

that might make it difficult for your friend. All I ask is that you understand the way it looks to an impartial police investigator."

Brittain consulted his notebook for what seemed like an age. Finally he looked up at Alice. "You have an outstanding record as an Annapolis midshipman, and you are well on your way to a career as a naval officer. I think you should do your duty and cooperate with the lawful authorities of the United States Department of Justice."

"Meaning you, I suppose?"

"Yes, you should cooperate with me."

"Even if I tend to incriminate myself? I am not required to answer any questions that might tend to incriminate me."

"Of course not, Lieutenant. But I'm not trying to incriminate you. I just want the facts."

Alice said nothing.

"I'll make a deal with you, Lieutenant. I won't ask you anything that might tend to incriminate you. Then you won't refuse to answer. Agreed?"

Alice fixed her eyes on Brittain's until his gaze shifted. "You can ask anything you want, Mr. Brittain. I don't have to answer."

"I know that, Lieutenant. I agree with that."

Alice said nothing.

"How do you think Frances Green knew there was a tape-recording device hidden in the living room of Marianne van Thuys's apartment?"

"Really! So the apartment was bugged!"

"It sure was. And we found the tape on Mrs. Green. The only tape in any of the rooms, by the way."

"Is there anything on the tape about Mrs. Green or me?"

Brittain hesitated. He felt he was gaining the cooperation of a key witness. He decided to tell her as much as he could without compromising the case for the prosecution.

"No, there's no mention of either of you. Actually, there's very little that could be construed as incriminating anybody. There was no reason for Mrs. Green to steal the cassette. The interesting question to me is this: What was she afraid *might* be on the tape that made her climb on that table and get it out of the ceiling smoke detector. What was she protecting herself against?"

Alice saw the opportunity to make a point. "Now, Mr. Brittain, I don't want to be antagonistic . . ."

"How could you possibly do that?" Brittain's irony was heavy.

Alice allowed herself to smile at the agent's gallows humor. "I don't want to be antagonistic," she repeated, "but maybe Frances Green had nothing to protect herself against because she isn't guilty of anything. Maybe your preconception that she is somehow involved in her husband's murder is creating problems you feel you have to solve."

"That's a gallant defense of your friend, Lieutenant. But you can't ignore one fact. Frances Green did go to the van Thuys apartment, and I found her there, gun in hand, near the dead body of her husband's mistress. And she did fire a shot. Now that's not a figment of my imagination."

"All she did was take the tape."

"Well, that's already obstruction of justice. But I'm sure she'll get off if she only wanted to destroy a record of her husband and his mistress. Maybe she had no clear idea of what she was doing. Maybe she was afraid of being recorded in the act of murder she was about to commit."

"Mr. Brittain, Frances Green did not kill her husband or his mistress. You would realize that if you knew her as well as I do."

"Possibly. But as of now, Frances Green is a prime suspect. And you yourself are under suspicion of being her accomplice, at least in the van Thuys murder."

"You've been threatening me, Mr. Brittain," Alice said. "Let's drop the nonsense and get to the real question. What exactly is on the tape?"

"Nothing, really. That's the funny thing. There are a few sweet nothings between lovers. There is no doubt about Green's intimate relations with van Thuys. But Green wasn't there for that."

"What was he there for?"

"You won't believe this, Lieutenant."

"Try me."

"They talked about economics."

"What kind of economics? Have you any idea?"

Brittain grinned. "That's pretty sharp, Lieutenant. You probably think I don't know a thing about economics. But the fact is, Sal Dannunzio got me interested in it after you got him interested. So, I took a few notes from the tape. Here is one thing Admiral Green said. Quote: 'There must be some long-term natural rate of unemployment reflecting people coming and going, plants closing and retooling, and all that. I'm sure there could be other short-term disturbances resulting from changes in the money supply that could increase or decrease unemployment. But in the long run I think the market forces of supply and demand will work, and unemployment will tend to settle around its natural rate.' Unquote. Rather dry talk for lovers, wouldn't you say?"

"For once we agree, Mr. Brittain. Is Marianne van Thuys just as dry on the tape?"

"She sure is. Here's her reply. Quote. 'You have to have faith in the market to adjust an excess supply of labor, just as you would an excess supply of grain or cars.' Unquote."

"Anything else?"

"Well, here's Marianne van Thuys being very emphatic. Quote. 'Inflation is everywhere a monetary phenomenon.' Unquote. Sounds like she's giving a professor back what she heard at his lectures. But Green doesn't sound like a professor. He ends by saying this. Quote. 'I'm convinced you're right, Marianne. But I will also make rational expectations part of the package.' Unquote. There's one interesting point about this tape."

"What's that?"

"From the sound of a Gershwin concert on the radio in the background, it's possible to get a fix on the date. It was Sunday morning, a few hours before Admiral Green was shot."

16

Motives for Murder

The interrogation of Alice Ritter ended as John Ritter arrived with a lawyer. Because no charges were filed, Alice and Frances Green were released. But they received a warning to remain in Washington where the authorities could find them. The Ritters and Frances Green drove back to the Green home.

Huddling together for comfort, they sat in the room where Frances Green had held grand social gatherings of the beautiful people, the cream of intellectual society in the nation's capital. The contrast struck all three of them, and they could not help remembering how discomfited Admiral Green had been by those parties at which he felt so out of place.

Thoughts about the past did not linger. Both women could be facing charges of murder, conspiracy, and obstruction of justice. Their harrowing experience left them emotionally exhausted.

"Alice, I'm sorry I got you into this," Frances broke the silence. "If I hadn't had the bright idea of going for the tape, this would never have happened."

"Forget it, Frances. I could have refused to go with you. If Marianne hadn't been shot, who knows, maybe your plan would have worked. We'll never know."

"That's big of you, Alice," said Frances appreciatively.

"I guess neither of you noticed Brittain tailing you when you drove into Washington," John Ritter commented.

"No, we didn't," Alice told him. "We were talking about the murder. We were too intent on that to think of anything else. We never thought to keep an eye on the rearview mirror."

"I wouldn't have noticed anything behind us anyway,"

Frances confessed. "I was too upset by the thought of seeing her. I presume Brittain will want an indictment for murder in the first degree. He already thought I was the prime suspect in Harry's murder. Now he thinks he's got me dead to rights in the van Thuys murder. A vindictive wife getting her revenge on her philandering husband and his paramour! And trying to shoot the FBI agent who arrested her! How will that sound to a jury?"

"And he's sure of his case against me as your accomplice," Alice pointed out. "He's sure I helped you. I was at the scene of the crime both times. Don't forget that."

John Ritter was as cheerful as possible. "Well, it's all circumstantial evidence. The burden of proof is on the prosecution."

"Sometimes circumstantial evidence is all that's needed for a guilty verdict," Alice reminded him. "We all know that."

"Don't be too pessimistic, Alice," her father urged. "It's not like you—not like smart, carefree Lieutenant Ritter. I'd say the best thing so far is that you both kept your heads cool and your mouths shut. You didn't get scared and talk more than you should have."

Frances felt the force of the compliment. "Thanks, John. I kept thinking how Harry used to tell me how hard it was for prisoners of war to give simply their name, rank, and serial number and nothing else. The human tendency to babble is overwhelming, especially under stress. That's why I made sure I didn't tell Brittain anything but my name. Alice, you did even better. You got information out of Brittain."

Alice smiled wanly. "Sort of interrogating the interrogator, is that what you mean?"

John Ritter patted her shoulder. "However you put it, you know some of what's on that tape, maybe enough to let us get a handle on this situation. We've been close to these murders. Could be, we can help solve them."

"I can see a little daylight at this point," Alice answered. "I can tell you something about the content of the tape from what Britain said. But I don't know who installed the recording device and fooled me into tipping them off about Admiral

141

Green's visits to Marianne. How could I have been so stupid as to fall for the story phony Commander Stock handed me? I could at least have checked with navy intelligence."

"Isn't it time you stopped beating your breast and started using your head, Alice?" her father asked. "Navy intelligence doesn't tell the names of their agents to every lieutenant who asks. What you've got to do is consider this question: Why was the admiral discussing economics with this woman? Isn't that an unlikely topic under the circumstances? Doesn't that give us a clue?"

"Isn't that obvious?" Frances put in. "Marianne must have been a good listener." Then somewhat wryly she added, "By profession."

"That's true, of course, but if they were discussing economics as Brittain said," Alice replied, "she was not just a passive listener." Then after a pause she added, "Frances, it's not really accurate to think of van Thuys as a prostitute—as merely a sex object. I know it's painful to acknowledge, but she had a great deal of worldly experience in business and financial matters. Her father was a pretty savvy operator in Indonesia and in Holland."

John Ritter added to the chain of thought. "They must have been discussing the issues Harry had to face in deciding between economic policies in the present crisis."

"They were," his daughter replied.

"Look," Frances exclaimed, "since we didn't commit either of these murders, who did? And why? I think they were political crimes—motivated by a desire to determine the country's economic policy."

"Do people kill for that?" John Ritter asked.

Alice spoke very quietly now. "The leaders of both sides in the debate viewed themselves as soldiers fighting for the safety of the country. In fact, they actually said they would do whatever was necessary to defend the United States from disaster."

"I think that's a reasonable motive for murder," Frances said. "I can see why some crazy economist would want Harry out of the way. But why Marianne van Thuys?"

"That's a tough one," John Ritter admitted. "Where is the economic tie between the two murders?"

"I can say this much," Alice offered. "Almost to the last, the admiral was undecided between the two economic strategies. He saw the sense in Sokolow's solution of responding to the immediate short-run problems of unemployment and restoration of confidence by stimulating demand. At the same time, he saw Christopherson's point about the long-run dangers of expansionary monetary policy."

"So that was what was on his mind while we were standing on the bridge on the *Chesapeake* during the storm!" Ritter inferred. "I'll bet Marianne van Thuys was part of the decision-making process. She must have been influencing him."

"Maybe she was being paid to influence him," Frances added tartly. "I know enough about our finances to know that Harry wasn't giving her enough money to keep her in the style to which she was accustomed."

John Ritter coughed apologetically. "Even assuming he gave her the money he took from our apartment deal," he said, "it wouldn't have been enough to keep her going. She must have been getting her income from somebody else."

Getting away from a distasteful subject, Frances went on, "Even if we knew which way she wanted him to go, whoever shot Harry had to know what he actually was going to do. So there are two questions. One is the nature of the van Thuys influence, and the other is Harry's own decision. Don't you see it that way, John?"

"Yes, I do. If we can find out who was keeping Marianne van Thuys, we should be a long way toward solving this mystery. Whoever planted the tape may have known the answer to your first question, Frances. And he may well have murdered Harry if he discovered the answer to the second. He acted before the admiral had a chance to report to the cabinet meeting on Sunday. Which brings us back to Alice, Brittain, and the tape. What's on it, Alice?"

His daughter gave a detailed description of her interrogation by Robert Brittain.

"The excerpts from the tape he read to me had Admiral Green saying he believed the best way to attack unemployment was to let supply and demand work freely. Marianne van Thuys mentioned the natural rate of unemployment and said flatly, 'Inflation is everywhere a monetary phenomenon.' Where have we heard that before?"

"From the Fed chairman," Frances answered. "Harcourt told me he heard Mr. Christopherson use that phrase many times."

"It sounds like Harry and Marianne agreed on some version of the market-oriented policies Christopherson or his associates have been pushing," John Ritter added.

"Correct," Alice said. "But it's not just a guess. At the end, Admiral Green said she had convinced him, and that he would put her ideas into the package. He must have been referring to his report to the President and the cabinet.

"You can see what that means. Marianne pressed the Federal Reserve arguments on Admiral Green. And he ended up saying he would advocate their position as a policy for the nation in the present economic crisis. It was plainly on this tape, so it must have been at least hinted at on the previous tapes. Somebody retrieved them from her apartment and listened to them."

As Alice talked, a pattern began to form in her mind. "I think I've got it," she said at the end.

"You mean you can tell who did the shooting?" Frances gasped.

"No. I'm not clear about that. But one thing is for sure. We've been discussing the *motive* of whoever did it. We should have been discussing *motives*. Plural. Everything makes sense once you realize that the motive for Admiral Green's murder was quite different than that for Marianne's murder."

"I don't follow you," her father protested.

"I've got an idea of what Alice is saying," Frances replied. "Harry could have been shot by a crazy economist, while Marianne was the victim of a crime of passion committed by a jealous admirer driven insane by the men who shared her. Two different motives for murder!"

"Let's go over the clues and see how they fit," Alice suggested.

She went back to the time Green was appointed the President's chief of staff, and their first conversations in the White House about the nation's financial crisis. She mentioned Green's meetings with economists on both sides of the debate, his meetings with Marianne van Thuys, and the tense situation aboard the *Chesapeake*. The events of that Sunday morning followed—Green's phone calls to Alice from the Pentagon, her calls to economists, and her call to Marianne.

"There it is!" Frances Green intervened in an excited voice. "You say you heard a man's voice in her apartment. He must be the one who killed her. Who was he?"

Alice shook her head. "I don't know. He was too far away from the phone. But I'm sure he wasn't Murray Sokolow or Martin Christopherson or anyone else I know well. There was something familiar, as if I'd heard it somewhere, maybe over the phone. But I just couldn't place it. However, he might be on the tape."

John Ritter shrugged. "This man could have committed both murders in a jealous rage. We may have been barking up the wrong tree in looking for an economist. We'll have to hear the tape and see if we can identify him."

"I'm sure Brittain won't let us hear it," Alice commented. "He's holding it until we are indicted."

"How was it———" Frances Green started to ask when the harsh ring of the telephone jarred the trio out of their intense concentration. She reached for the phone after the second ring.

"Hello."

The voice on the other end was inaudible to the Ritters.

"Oh, hello Mrs. Wedik. Yes, I'll call you Mildred. All right."

Frances sat down with the phone and listened to a long discourse on the other end.

During the silence, Alice was thinking hard about the clues in the case. Suddenly all the factors fell into place, and she saw the solution she was looking for. She glanced up as Frances said, "No, Mildred, there's no need to apologize."

The voice at the other end said something.

"No, no, Mrs. Wedik," Frances protested, "I don't hold you responsible for what happened."

Mrs. Wedik persisted at the other end.

"Well, Mildred, it's all over now."

Mildred was obviously being penitent.

"It's over and done with, Mildred. No, I can't think how you could help. Wait, Mildred, Alice Ritter wants to say something."

Alice took the phone. "Hello, Mrs. Wedik. I believe there is something very important you can do for Mrs. Green."

Alice explained what she wanted, received an affirmative reply, and set down the phone.

Then she laid out her solution of the case for Frances Green and her father. They both looked mesmerized long before she finished her analysis.

17
Who the Mystery Woman Is

It was long after midnight when the Ritters left the Green home. Alice got a few hours of sleep, and by morning she was ready for the meeting with the President that she had arranged over the phone with the First Lady. She reached the White House on time and found Wedik looking better than she had seen him since the financial crisis struck.

"He's got himself under control," she thought. "Thank goodness for that."

As if reading her mind, Wedik explained the reason. "The economic package we put together is having a good effect. It's a bit of Keynesianism and a bit of monetarism. I don't claim the compromise is better than coming down flatfooted on one side or the other, and I can't tell how long it's going to last. Sokolow and Christopherson are unanimous that it hasn't long to go. They both insist the combination is too unstable. Needless to say, Sokolow believes there are too many monetarist elements in it, and Christopherson believes the whole thing is too Keynesian.

"When I pointed out to Christopherson how monetarist we've been in holding the line on money growth, he argued with me that monetary restraint is not compatible with big federal defense spending outlays and tax cuts. When I mentioned to Sokolow how Keynesian we've been, he said, 'Mr. President, too little and too late! You need to get the Fed to expand the money supply or your tax cuts will simply raise the budget deficit.' "

Wedik pursed his lips. "I can't help that. I had to stop the wrangling and make a statement to the American people and to the world. And whatever the economists may say, that's what you need in politics. Make a decision, and show you believe in it!

"The compromise stopped the panic, eased the dollar hemorrhage, and kept the stock market from going through the floor once again. The country is in for a long haul. I agree that changes will have to be made along the way, but we've made a start. The news media know that. Their headlines aren't about the financial crisis so much now. They're about these two terrible murders."

"That's what I want to discuss with you, Mr. President," Alice said.

"Well, I hope you have some useful ideas, Lieutenant. I've been trying to stay as far away from the investigation as possible. My answer to questions from the newshounds is always the same. 'The FBI is making substantial progress in the case.' I only wish it were true!"

The President and the lieutenant paused in their conversation, thinking about the field day the Sunday supplements were having with the romantic entanglement between Admiral Harcourt Green, the President's chief of staff, and Marianne van Thuys, the late courtesan-about-Washington. The papers were full of titillating stories expanding on the themes of lust, jealousy, violence, and corruption in high places. Television talk show hosts reveled in gallows humor. Evangelists took a stern moral tone with the administration, and called on public officials to repent of their sins.

"Most people seem to think Frances Green is guilty," Wedik said.

"Frances isn't guilty, and I can prove it," Alice replied. "They're also saying my father and I were involved because we stand to gain financially from Admiral Green's death. That isn't true either, and I can prove that, too."

Wedik gave her a quizzical stare. "What is the truth, then?"

"Just this, Mr. President."

Alice spoke to him as she had spoken to Frances Green and John Ritter the night before, listing the suspects and the clues, describing the thread she had found that led her through the maze to the exit—the solution.

Wedik was as amazed at the end as the others had been. At last he managed to say, "I'll get the FBI on to this right away!"

"Not yet, Mr. President," Alice advised him. "The FBI might have a hard time proving its case. Give me the opportunity, and I'll give them all the evidence they need."

"You make more sense than anyone on the case," the President admitted. "I might as well go along with you a little further at least. What do you want?"

"A voyage."

"A voyage?"

"Not very far, Mr. Wedik. Just the *Chesapeake* down the Potomac with these guests aboard."

Alice took a slip of paper from her purse and held it out. Wedik accepted the paper and examined the list. He mulled over the names in silence.

"Can you get them all aboard ship this afternoon?" Alice inquired.

"No problem. But why do you want to do it like this?"

"No one will suspect anything if they're all invited to a voyage with the President and the First Lady. That should make it easier to startle somebody into a confession. With a bit of luck, the whole case may be solved. Besides, on a ship there's no place to run and hide when the truth comes out."

"All right! That's the way we'll do it!" the President said emphatically. "I'll give you every chance to prove you're right!"

And so it happened that at two in the afternoon, the *Chesapeake* slipped away from the dock and headed into the Potomac carrying all those Alice had named. The host and hostess and their guests were seated in the main lounge of the converted cruiser. Chief John Ritter was on the bridge.

President Wedik looked around the group. "I think you all know each other. Have a drink while we talk."

As Alice had urged, the President was treating this as a social occasion, ignoring the deadly antagonisms he knew divided his guests.

Seated next to Murray Sokolow and Howard Tilson were the chief FBI investigator, Robert Brittain, and Sal Dannunzio. Then came Martin Christopherson of the Federal Reserve and Alan Claus, flanked by Mildred Wedik, who placed herself close to Frances Green as if to lend her moral support. Alice Ritter sat opposite the President. She sat erect in her chair, tense and solemn.

The President was almost jovial. "Lieutenant Ritter, would you be good enough to share with these folks the ideas you've already presented to me? I'm sure they would be interested."

Alice's mouth was dry. "Yes sir. Now————"

The President interrupted. "Now, Alice, maybe we should make it clear how we feel about all these fine patriotic public servants who are here."

The *Chesapeake* nosed out into the channel, and Alice could see the shoreline moving past through the saloon ports. The ship was gathering speed as it cleared the last landfalls.

"As I was saying, everyone in this room holds his—or her," Wedik smiled at Alice—"duty to the safety and well-being of the United States above everything else."

"Yes sir————" Alice began again.

"Above everything else," the President reiterated. "That means above life itself. The people here are soldiers in the defense of their country. Mrs. Wedik and I have talked about this many times. Haven't we, dear?"

Mildred opened her mouth as if to speak but managed only an affirmative nod before her husband continued.

"Yes, good soldiers in defense of the safety of their country. Soldiers willing to do whatever is necessary to protect America. Even if it's painful—even if they suffer for it." The President paused. "Even if they have to inflict pain on others, even if death is the result." Wedik's captive audience shifted uneasily in their seats as he continued his peroration. "Such is the lot of the soldier. He must do his duty as he sees it, or she sees it, whatever the cost."

150

"Yes, sir————" Alice made another attempt, only to be thwarted by Wedik again. His volubility gave her a queasy feeling that he was becoming psychologically unstuck again. His next words increased her concern.

"Whatever the cost, I say. Look around this room. There is Mr. Brittain and Mr. Dannunzio of the FBI. Dedicated public servants. Fearless and dogged in their performance of their duty. Take Lieutenant Ritter, who, like all service men and women, has taken an oath to protect the United States 'against all enemies whomsoever.' There is Dr. Sokolow and his colleague, Professor Tilson. Dr. Sokolow was in the armed services so he took the same oath. But more important, he is a servant of the Congress and the President as chairman of the Council of Economic Advisers. He is a civilian, but he is just as responsible a soldier as when he was on active duty."

Wedik would not stop. "Look at Mr. Christopherson over there. He defends the money supply and the value of the dollar against all its enemies whomsoever. A true soldier in the defense of the sound economy of the United States. Yes. A true soldier ready to do what needs to be done."

Abruptly, the President rose and walked directly over to the chairman of the Federal Reserve system. He stood over him only a few inches away. "That is right, isn't it, Mr. Christopherson—Martin? May I call you Martin?"

The banker was startled. "Yes, sir. Of course you may call me Martin."

"Are you a good soldier, Martin? Do you do your duty no matter what the consequences? Do you?" The President leaned forward almost face to face with the banker.

"Yes, sir. Yes, that is the way I feel about my work."

Quickly, almost nimbly for a man of his bulk, Wedik stepped away and stood over Sokolow. "And you, Murray? Where do you stand?"

Sokolow rose from his chair, forcing the President to straighten up. The men were face to face, inches apart. "You know how I feel, Mr. President. I have been fighting for an end to unemployment and poverty all my life. Since the Depression years, in the university and in politics, I have been fighting for the right causes." Then, after a momentary pause, "I have been the kind of person you describe as a soldier longer than anyone here—including you, Mr. President, if I may say so."

"Call me Stanley, won't you?" Then, turning to the hypnotized assembly, "All you good soldiers, call me Stanley. Now go on, Alice."

Relieved that the President was able to stop babbling, Alice spoke quickly to prevent him from beginning again.

"All right—Stanley—my duty is to tell the whole truth. Isn't it, sir?" This time it was Alice who did not pause for a reply. "Well, Mrs. Green, my father, and I are all suspects in the murder of Admiral Green and Marianne van Thuys. That's only natural. All three of us could be considered as having motives. I don't doubt that Mr. Brittain has been thinking along these lines, and I don't blame him."

The FBI agent protested. "We haven't charged any one of you three, Lieutenant."

"It's not necessary to use that sort of talk with me. If I were you, I would come to the same conclusion. But we three, who are the likely candidates of routine police methods, know we are not guilty. This is what permitted us to take a different tack and deduce who committed the murders."

"So you know who is responsible, Alice?" The President broke in.

"Yes, sir, I do. And if you will give me a chance, I'll explain my reasoning to you."

"Go ahead. We have time and this is the ideal place to have it out."

The group followed the President's gaze to the portholes. The *Chesapeake* was pushing out to sea. Against the hull, the roughening waves slapped out a faster tempo than in the safe confines of the harbor.

"We're dealing with two different murders and two different motives," Alice began. "There's a personal connection we all know about between the two victims. I'm sorry to go into this again, Frances."

152

"Lay it all out, Alice," Mrs. Green replied. "I'm aware of all the facts, and I'm reconciled to them. Nothing you reveal will bother me now."

Alice nodded sympathetically. She resumed her analysis of the case.

"Marianne van Thuys was Admiral Green's mistress. Any solution has to explain why these two suffered the same fate. The obvious answer—it would occur to anyone looking at the facts—is that they were victims of a crime of passion. Somebody shot Admiral Green out of jealousy and Marianne van Thuys for revenge. Or vice versa, depending on whether the criminal was a man or a woman."

Brittain spoke tactfully, carefully avoiding Frances Green's name. "But Lieutenant, you've insisted all along that nobody here, who might fit your description, actually did it."

"Well, what about somebody who isn't here?"

Sokolow and Christopherson looked thoughtful.

The chairman of the Fed spoke first. "Yes. I agree. I never thought one of this gathering could be the criminal."

"Neither did I," Sokolow added. "Lieutenant, I see your point. You wanted us here so we could learn all at once that there's no murderer among us."

Brittain spoke disgustedly. "Then this little drama is *Hamlet* without the Prince of Denmark. You'd better tell us who it is, Lieutenant Ritter. I can call ashore and have the criminal arrested."

"There's no need to hurry," Alice replied. "The person I'm thinking about is not suspicious and won't run away. Besides, I want to see if we all agree about where the clues point."

"Okay, give us the clues," Dannunzio suggested.

Alice continued. "Granted that this was a crime of passion, we have a prime suspect—a mystery woman who came to the attention of the White House Secret Service through an anonymous informant. She and Admiral Green used to have assignations at a motel near Baltimore. She's described by the manager of the motel as a tall brunette. This affair took place when the admiral was stationed at the naval procurement office of the Norfolk Naval Station. It so happens that a tall brunette was working there at the same time. It says so in a Commerce Department brochure.

"Then the admiral was transferred to Washington and began his affair with Marianne van Thuys. Anyone might suspect that here we have a motive for murder."

Tilson shook his head. "That's all pretty hypothetical."

"There's more," Alice told him. "This mystery woman grew up on a farm in Iowa. She used to do a lot of shooting, so she knows how to handle a rifle, which means————"

Tilson was dumbfounded. "You can't mean Jerry!"

Alice nodded. "Geraldine Anderson. But there's more to go on. Admiral Green consulted all the economists who could help him. He wanted different opinions. Geraldine Anderson is a prominent supply-side economist. Yet he avoided her. That suggests he had a personal motive. A broken romance would explain it."

"But they only met," Tilson protested, "when I brought her to the party at his home."

Alice had her rejoinder ready. "That's what she told you. She wanted to meet him again, and maybe this was the first chance she had, even if his wife was present. As for the admiral, he must have been staggered when he saw the supply-side economist you brought to the party."

Alice paused. Nobody said anything. Some faces were puzzled, others expectant, still others impassive. Frances Green touched a handkerchief to the corner of her eye.

Alice gazed around the circle before continuing. "The final incriminating evidence suggesting the guilt of Geraldine Anderson concerns the Sunday when the admiral was shot. When he phoned from the Pentagon, he told me he had finished his report. When I got to the Pentagon, he had left a message saying he wasn't finished yet. This contradiction didn't seem like much at the time, but it does now.

"Geraldine Anderson was at the Pentagon that morning. I

saw her come out—and she looked absolutely furious. We can guess why. Admiral Green didn't go to the Pentagon to finish his report, he went there to meet her, and to tell her that their affair was over and done with. Of course, it was not a pleasant discussion, and if he could not cut it short as he had planned, that would explain his contradictory messages about finishing his report. He needed more time to deal with her than he expected."

"Well, there's no difficulty about why Admiral Green was shot," Sokolow said. "Your explanation makes sense."

"But how did she do it?" Christopherson asked.

"Well, she knew Admiral Green would be driving from the Pentagon to the White House," Alice explained. "And she came out of the Pentagon before he did. No doubt he was giving her time to get out of sight so they wouldn't be seen together. She could have driven to the National Academy of Sciences, hidden behind the juniper bush, and been prepared for the assassination when his car arrived."

Brittain stood up. "Mr. President, with your permission I'll call ashore and have Geraldine Anderson arrested on a charge of murder in the first degree."

Wedik looked at Alice Ritter.

"Sit down, Mr. Brittain," Alice said. "I don't think you'll be arresting Geraldine Anderson."

"Why not?"

"Because she's not guilty."

"How do you know that?"

"Since she went to the Pentagon to meet Admiral Green, she must have been hoping to restore their old relationship. So, she had no reason to bring a weapon with her. And anyway, it wouldn't have been a rifle. It would have been a handgun.

"Besides, she couldn't have known about Marianne van Thuys. She probably suspected there was another woman, but Admiral Green wouldn't have told her who it was. Geraldine had no motive to murder Marianne."

155

Brittain sat down. "What an anticlimax," he said sourly. "Why get us all together just to tell us a lurid tale?"

"I never said Geraldine Anderson was guilty," Alice pointed out. "I just said she was the mystery woman of the case. I went through this scenario to eliminate responsibility and focus on where we have to go. I hope we're all comfortable. We have a lot more to talk about."

18

The Short Run

Quiet fell over the *Chesapeake's* main lounge. All those present were communing with their thoughts. They seemed to be reflecting about what Alice had said, and wondering about what was to come. Mildred Wedik placed her hand sympathetically on Frances Green's arm. Brittain whispered something to Dannunzio, who nodded. Sokolow, Christopherson, Tilson, and Claus stared straight ahead.

Alice waited until they appeared ready for her to go on.

"When we say Geraldine Anderson did not commit these murders," she said, "we also say this was not a crime of passion because there is no other suspect with jealousy or revenge for a motive. So, we have to go back to the beginning and consider these two murders from a different point of view.

"Let's consider the murder of Admiral Green first. What kind of crime was it? The answer is that it was a crime committed by the kind of soldier President Wedik mentioned. It was a political crime designed to determine the economic policy of the United States, because the murderer believed he was saving the country from the ruin that would result if Admiral Green proposed a program he believed would be a disaster."

"You needn't be tactful, Alice" the President interrupted. "We all know that I was prepared to take Green's word. I'm in better command of myself now. Go on. I've talked too much already. The floor is yours."

"All right, Mr. President. The admiral was going to make policy for all practical purposes. That was no secret to either Dr. Sokolow or Mr. Christopherson. The admiral met with them in private conferences————"

"In your presence," Wedik prompted.

"Yes, sir, in my presence. These meetings were designed to allow each side in the debate on government policy in the economic crisis to present its case."

"Did anyone succeed in convincing him, Lieutenant Ritter?" Wedik queried.

The President, self-controlled once again, was acting like an effective lawyer questioning a witness to bring out the strong points in her favor. It was hard to imagine that he was the same impotent figure who had turned the affairs of state over to his chief of staff in a panic at being unable to make up his mind.

"I'll come to my point in a minute, Mr. President," Alice replied.

"So what were the issues?" Dannunzio asked. The younger FBI agent was intrigued by her.

"Mr. Dannunzio, they all boiled down to a question of whether we believe we ought to deal with the immediate emergency of unemployment, and all the loss of confidence and panic that entails, or whether we feel that the instruments to deal with the short-run situation will lead to worse, even catastrophic, long-run problems."

"Who was on which side?"

Alice looked at the four economists in the room in turn. "I'm sure the professionals here could say more elegantly than I what was involved. But I'll try to put it in a nutshell."

"You're doing fine," Sokolow grunted. Christopherson nodded agreement.

"Well, Dr. Sokolow and Professor Tilson are Keynesians who believe that continued unemployment, and the flood of bankruptcies that follow from a tight money supply, will bring about a collapse. Therefore, at whatever cost, it's necessary to institute a program of government spending, financed by increased supplies of money, to combat the contraction."

"And we're right," Sokolow said. "Increased production will eventually match the supply of goods to the increased demand, so inflation will ease."

Alice accepted the interruption to let him make his point. "Mr. Christopherson and Professor Claus," she noted, "believe that, on the contrary, these short-run policies would lead to massive inflation in the future as the money supply is, as they put it, recklessly expanded."

"Professor Claus and I aren't in complete agreement about monetarism," Christopherson put in. "I say that people will adapt themselves to rising inflation by forming habits that are hard to break. Inflationary expectations tend to continue, and can be counteracted only by hard deflationary policies."

Claus shrugged. "Well, I'm a 'new classical economist,' and so I believe people use all the information available to them. They anticipate and discount government policies. But I believe like Mr. Christopherson that government policies are often wrongheaded and badly timed. Attempts to fine-tune the economy only decrease reliable information and confuse business decision makers. Laissez-faire is my watchword. The market will come back to equilibrium of its own accord."

"Monetarism is the problem," Sokolow interrupted. Rigidity in the money supply means that when demand for money varies, interest rates will fluctuate drastically. Flexibility is the right policy."

"So-called flexibility is the wrong policy!" Christopherson snapped. "The demand for money is stable in the long run, and must be met by a stable money supply."

"Events proved you wrong!" Sokolow retorted heatedly. "The velocity of money—the demand for it—has jumped all over the place. Your rigidity in supply has given us volatile interest rates and all the bad effects on the stock market and the value of the dollar."

Alice followed the interchange, and when it ended she continued. "Of course, practical politicians can't always stick to one theory. The previous administration used monetarism, supply-side thinking, and rational expectations at different times. In the past, the big budget deficit came about because of tax cuts along with increased spending on military buildup. I'm sensitive to that last point—we in the navy understand the need for new ships. And of course there were large domestic programs that had to be funded."

Claus intervened. "Since Jerry Anderson has been mentioned, and since she's not here to defend her supply-side economics, I think we should note that she expected the budget deficit to disappear as tax *rate* cuts increased the GNP and therefore the tax *take*. The ironic thing was that just when she was urging monetary and fiscal expansion, some liberal Keynesians were warning of demand-pull inflation and calling for higher taxes and less military spending. That was before this new round of unemployment, which sent them back to advocating expansion again."

Dannunzio intervened. "So it's fair to say that, as far as Green could see, we were damned if we dealt with short-run problems by the arguments of the monetarists, and damned if we didn't deal with them by the arguments of the Keynesians." Apparently carried away by Alice's reasoning, he glanced sheepishly at the other participants.

"Then Green could not make up his mind," Sokolow commented. "I suspected as much."

Alice shook her head. "No, Dr. Sokolow. The admiral was not a man to let anything drift, least of all important decisions. He made up his mind, and he would never have waited for the morning of the cabinet meeting to do so. After all, he had the essential facts when he was aboard this ship for the last time. It's my belief he knew then what he would do, although he carefully avoided saying so. Of course, he kept gathering more information, but I'm sure it merely confirmed him in the judgment he had made."

Dannunzio was following the line of thought of the young naval officer so intensely that he could not refrain from interrupting to make a point for her. "Lieutenant, whoever shot the admiral had to know what he was going to do, and had to be determined to prevent him from doing it."

The President turned to Christopherson abruptly. "You would stop Green if it meant the whole future of the country, wouldn't you?"

The banker was taken aback by the sudden force of the question. "I didn't shoot Green!" he expostulated.

"But he would do it," Sokolow interposed. "Of course he

would if he thought the whole future of the country was at stake. It would be like somebody able to prevent World War Three—saving the lives of millions at the expense of one."

"I did not assassinate Admiral Green!" Christopherson exploded. "What I would do is a purely hypothetical question! I did not shoot Harcourt Green! I did not conspire to have him shot!"

"No, Mr. Christopherson," Alice interjected, "you did not shoot the admiral because he was going to advocate the substance of your policy."

Sokolow paled. "How can you know that, Lieutenant?" Before Alice could reply, he added, "And how could Christopherson know what Green was going to do?"

"The answer is obvious—Marianne van Thuys," Alice responded. "I was in a position in which I knew of Admiral Green's meetings with this woman. Perhaps I should have realized it earlier from remarks he dropped, but in any case I now know that Marianne was feeding him the monetarist position."

"How can you possibly know that?" This time it was the Federal Reserve chairman who was shaken by her conclusions.

"It's clear from a tape that was taken from Marianne's apartment, Mr. Christopherson. Mr. Brittain has the tape. He told me some of what was on it. Marianne can be heard pushing monetarist policies, and the admiral can be heard saying he agrees with her."

"Can you give us some examples, Alice?" the President prompted.

"Yes, sir, I can. Marianne speaks of a natural rate of unemployment. That's a monetarist concept. It's basic to the belief expressed by Professor Milton Friedman of the University of Chicago that monetary policy cannot influence 'real' components of the economy for any extended period of time."

"You mean," Wedik said, "that changes in the money supply will change the overall price level?"

Sokolow intervened impatiently. "Friedman says that's true of the long run, but even he admits it will raise employment in the short run. Employment depends on aggregate demand. Full employment doesn't come about automatically."

"Come now, Dr. Sokolow," Wedik protested, "this is not the time to argue the merits of these positions."

"Sorry, Mr. President," Sokolow responded to the rebuke. "It's just that I feel so strongly about these issues. The whole nation is at stake, the whole world!"

The President prevented him from speaking further. "I know how you feel about waiting for the long run. Let's wait now and listen to Lieutenant Ritter."

"The tape has another comment by Marianne van Thuys— 'inflation is everywhere a monetary phenomenon'—which is also a monetarist catch phrase," Alice said.

"Is it, Mr. Christopherson?" the President demanded.

Christopherson was on the defensive, but he conceded that monetarism argued from the stable demand for money to the conclusion that any additional money supply would raise prices. The quantity of money was sufficient to explain all price changes, inflationary or deflationary.

Sokolow could not contain himself. "If that's true at all it's only true in the long run. In the short run, where we all live, the demand for money is highly variable. Inflation is much more complicated. Sometimes it's caused by excessive demand—for many reasons, of which changes in the money supply may or may not be an important one. Sometimes it's caused by cost-push elements like higher wages or petroleum prices."

"Mr. Sokolow," Wedik said, "please sit down and control yourself."

The distracted professor perched himself on the edge of his chair, his crossed legs twitching in little kicklike motions. Lighting a cigarette gave him something to do with his hands. He only managed a puff or two before crushing it out.

Alice carried on. "The point is that van Thuys was earning her living this way. Frances pointed out that Admiral Green was not providing her with any substantial amount of cash—at least not enough to maintain that apartment in Georgetown, not to speak of keeping her in expensive clothes and all that.

She was no expert on macroeconomics. She got her ideas—and her money—from somebody else. A monetarist. Everything points to that."

"So it was Christopherson who really kept her," Sokolow crowed. "You put her up to poisoning Green's mind!" Sokolow's finger pointed like a dagger at his counterpart from the Fed.

Before Christopherson could answer, Dannunzio broke in to say that he had already begun an investigation of the van Thuys finances. "It won't take long to trace down the source of her funds, no matter how carefully laundered."

"Marianne van Thuys was on my payroll!" Christopherson decided to brazen it. "She was not the first or the last consultant that a federal agency has hired to present its case."

"A whore consultant—is that it?" Frances exploded. "You can say it even plainer than that, Christopherson. In plain words you admit to being a pimp . . . a procurer."

Flushing with fury, the banker faced the widow. "Call me whatever you want, Mrs. Green. I did what I had to do. If I had allowed these Keynesians to try one quick fix after another, the crisis would have gotten worse, and in the long run the country would have collapsed. God knows, we are close to that point already." The banker abandoned all pretense of professional reserve. "I'll tell you one thing, Mrs. Green, and that is I did not kill your husband! If anything, Lieutenant Ritter's argument shows that if Marianne was successful in her lobbying with Green, then the admiral would have come down on my side."

Alice intervened in a quiet but firm voice. "You're forgetting that we have a second crime to explain—the murder of Marianne van Thuys."

Christopherson fell silent as if chastened by a reprimand.

"How are the two murders connected?" Alice went on. "Answer: the tape. It was introduced surreptitiously into the smoke detector in her apartment."

"Why secretly?" Dannunzio inquired. "Maybe she knew about it."

Alice shook her head. "She would not have had to hide it in the smoke detector. The men who visited her would have had no suspicion they were being taped. She could have hidden it safely in a more accessible place like the telephone. Besides, there was no tape in the bedroom, the obvious place if her motive was blackmail. No, somebody got into her apartment secretly and planted the bug. Who was it?"

The members of Alice's audience stared at one another and then back at the speaker. They waited for her to resume her argument.

"The two murders were committed for two different motives, because there's no single motive that would serve as a connecting link between them. Now, who had one reason for shooting Admiral Green and another reason for shooting Marianne van Thuys?"

Alice had the floor to herself. The others listened, spellbound.

"About the tape, it was there in the smoke detector when Admiral Green visited Marianne on Sunday morning. That's how they were both recorded. But there's a third person on the tape, isn't there, Mr. Brittain?"

The FBI agent gulped and tried to say something. Alice cut him short. "There's no need to answer. I know. It's Howard Tilson."

Tilson started. "What are you saying?" he stammered.

"I'm saying that when I called Marianne on Sunday, I heard a man's voice in the background. I recognized the voice just now. It was yours. I'm doubly sure because I also listened to the taped conversation you had with Admiral Green."

An ugly red suffused Tilson's face. He tugged at his collar.

"You had the two motives," Alice challenged him. "As a Keynesian, you wanted the admiral dead. As Marianne's jealous, vindictive lover, you wanted both of them dead. You could have gone from Marianne's apartment to murder Green. Then, in a crazed frenzy, you could have gone back to the apartment two days later to murder her. You had motive, opportunity, the knowledge that Green was at the Pentagon, and familiarity with his habit of stopping at the Lincoln Memorial, which would bring him back to the White House by way of Bacon Drive. Of course, Marianne told you where he was on Sunday."

Tilson struggled to say something.

Sokolow shook his head sorrowfully. "You shouldn't have done it, Howard."

Tilson found his voice. "I didn't! I didn't! Sure, I was with Marianne when Green arrived on Sunday. I hid in her spare room. I never heard what they said. But I wasn't jealous of Marianne. I knew I wasn't the only man on her string, and it never bothered me! She was just a woman to have fun with!"

The others erupted into a storm of questions. Defensively, Tilson looked from one to the other, answering as best he could.

"Hold it!" Alice called out. Again she was greeted with silence.

"I know you're innocent," she addressed Tilson.

"What's that?" Claus demanded.

"Howard Tilson couldn't have planted the tape, or else he would have taken it from the apartment on Sunday morning. He could have retrieved it while Marianne was in the shower. Anyway, he wouldn't have allowed himself to be taped in her apartment in the first place. What if the tapes fell into the wrong hands?

"And we know that he could not have murdered Marianne van Thuys. The psychology wouldn't have been right. A man insane and homicidal with jealousy might have shot both Admiral Green and Marianne that same morning. He would not have let two days go by between the murders."

Brittain finally got a word in. "Lieutenant Ritter, Tilson's voice isn't on the tape."

Alice smiled. "I thought that might be the case. His voice was faint in the background, so I guess he was too far away from the bug. I said he was on the tape because I wanted to get his reaction. It's the reaction I expected. I know he's innocent."

"Thank you, Lieutenant!" Sokolow exclaimed. "I'm glad you've made that point. I'd never have gotten over it if a close colleague like Howard was guilty. But who is then?"

"Look at it this way, Dr. Sokolow. Admiral Green was shot by a Keynesian who knew how he was going to advise the President. He's the one who planted tapes in Marianne's apartment, or had them planted by a confederate.

"From the series of tapes, he must have known which way Admiral Green was tending. And the last tape he heard confirmed his worst suspicions. He heard the admiral tell Marianne van Thuys that he intended to push a monetarist solution at the cabinet meeting on Sunday. It must have been much the same message as on the tape found in Marianne's apartment."

"Where does that get us?" Claus asked.

"Well, there are just two Keynesians important enough for the admiral to consult personally, important enough to know how completely the President was relying on the admiral. One is Howard Tilson. The other . . ."

"You mean . . ." Claus started to say.

"It can't be!" Christopherson exclaimed.

But the pair turned, as did all the rest, to look at the chairman of the Council of Economic Advisors. Sokolow leaned back in his chair and moistened his lips with the tip of his tongue.

"You sent that phony Commander Stock to bamboozle me," Alice accused him.

Sokolow looked blankly around the circle of faces.

"Commander Stock is your henchman, isn't he? You got him to plant the tapes, activate them, and retrieve them, didn't you? I'm happy to say he's no commander. He isn't even in the navy."

Sokolow brushed his fingertips across his forehead. He tried to force himself to say something. "I'm . . . I'm . . ." That was as far as he could get.

Alice pressured him. "You might as well tell us Commander Stock's real name."

Sokolow gasped for breath while the others waited. At last he succeeded in mumbling. "Stock's real name is Simpson. He's a communications expert."

"We'll find Simpson and get his story," Brittain said. "Go on, Lieutenant Ritter. You're making a great case for us."

"Well, so-called Commander Stock received the message whenever I called the number he gave me and spoke the word 'Georgetown.' He knew what to do."

Dannunzio shook his head. "This is the first I've heard of that."

"Sorry I couldn't tell you, or Mr. Brittain either. But then, I was a suspect in your books. My Georgetown calls must have been recorded at Stock's—Simpson's—end. They alerted him to the fact that Admiral Green was on his way to Marianne's and he knew to trigger the bug in her apartment.

"But I'm sure he had nothing to do with the murder, did he, Dr. Sokolow? You couldn't trust that secret to anyone else, could you? Anyhow, you didn't need him. The Old Executive Office Building is close enough to the National Academy of Sciences for you to get easily from one to the other. My guess is, you had a rifle concealed in your car. You were coming and going on Sunday, so the guard took no note of the time when, instead or reporting to the White House, you drove to a place near the academy, carried your rifle onto the grounds, and hid behind the juniper. It wasn't difficult for you to draw a bead on Admiral Green and hit him with a single shot when we stopped for a red light. You learned to use a Springfield rifle in the service, didn't you?"

"I made expert on the rifle range," Sokolow confirmed her analysis. In different circumstances, it would have been a boast.

"I'm glad you didn't need a second shot," Alice told him. "I might have been your second victim. Well, you shot Admiral Green, ditched the rifle, knowing it couldn't be traced to you, went back to your car, and drove to your office. It seemed like the perfect crime—and the perfect way to put an end to the admiral's economic philosophy."

A trickle of sweat ran down Sokolow's face. He dabbed at it mechanically with his handkerchief. "The last tape Stock brought me was the final straw," he croaked. "From what

Green said, I knew he would doom the country to a monetarist program. You can see, can't you, that I had to remove him?"

Sokolow looked around as if expecting an approving answer. He seemed bewildered by the silence that greeted his question.

Alice went on. "Of course, you knew the last tape was still in the van Thuys apartment. You felt you couldn't take the chance of having Stock try to retrieve it, but then there wasn't any need to retrieve it. It couldn't be traced to you. You didn't need it, not with the admiral gone. And so-called Commander Stock would remain silent for fear of being prosecuted as your accomplice. It looked like you were home free."

Sokolow's eyes bulged. "I didn't need the last tape," he gasped. "It was Stock's idea to follow Green on Sunday and trigger the bug when he went to the van Thuys apartment."

"Then Stock went home," Alice inferred, "intending to return to the apartment when the coast was clear and retrieve the tape. Only you upset his plan by shooting Admiral Green."

The room was hushed. The vibrations of the ship's engine could be felt in the stillness like a pulse beat continuing after consciousness has been lost. They were like the final efforts of the heart of a dying man, his body reduced to this last minimal function before it too stopped in the total silence of death.

President Wedik spoke at last. "Is it necessary to take this any further, Dr. Sokolow?"

The answer came in a hoarse monosyllable. "No."

Sokolow sat slumped in his chair, inert. The company turned its attention to the young woman who had exposed him. Except for the quiet movement of Salvatore Dannunzio into position next to the confessed murderer, they continued as if Sokolow were not present.

"You really gave me a turn," Tilson told Alice. "That was the first I heard about the tape. I knew I could have been on it since I was in Marianne's apartment."

"Sorry, but while I knew you didn't commit murder, you still might have been an accomplice. That's why I staged my little drama with you in a leading role. My idea was to trick Sokolow into a confession that would explain everything to do with Admiral Green's murder.

"Frankly, it didn't matter whether you were on the tape or not. I just had to make you think you were—and make Sokolow think the same thing. That's why I cut Mr. Brittain short before he could give the game away."

Tilson grimaced. "It's funny to think you knew it wasn't me at all because I didn't take the tape from Marianne's apartment."

"Oh, I had better evidence than that. Your voice was a dead giveaway when I phoned Marianne on Sunday and heard you in the background."

"I don't get it. How did that get me off the hook?"

"When I hear a man calling a woman like Marianne van Thuys into the bedroom," said Alice dryly, "I figure he has something on his mind besides murder."

19
The Long Run

Brittain was complimentary. "You've cleared up the mystery, Lieutenant Ritter. Thanks for the assist."

"Now that you've exposed Sokolow," Dannunzio added, "we can take it from here."

Alice shook her head. "Not quite. Remember, we've got two murders to solve. We've only solved one. Dr. Sokolow killed Admiral Green, but he did not kill Marianne van Thuys. He had no motive for the second shooting. We have to find out who did, and who pulled the trigger. We need a second motive."

"What can you tell us about that?" Wedik prompted her to go on.

"First of all, Marianne knew the person who murdered her," Alice replied. "When Frances and I got to the apartment house shortly after the shooting, the outer door was ajar and the door to her apartment was unlocked. Either she let her visitor in, or somebody had two keys."

"My husband did," said Frances bitterly. "I saw him unlock the outer door. Marianne must have given him a key to her own door. I understand that's how men call on women in her profession."

"Before anyone else says it for me," Tilson interjected, "I'll own up to having two keys to Marianne's building."

"Commander Stock—I'd better stop calling him that—must have had two keys, too," Alice observed, "because he had to get in and out to plant and retrieve the tapes. It wouldn't have been feasible for him to break and enter every time. He must have watched her apartment. When Marianne went out, he went in by simply unlocking the doors. He took the old tape and left a new one."

"Are you claiming he shot her?" Claus inquired.

"No, Professor. He wasn't close to her. He had no personal motive. And Dr. Sokolow has told us he's a communications expert. So he had no economic or political motive either, even if he had been within the highest circles of government, which he wasn't."

"Where do we go from here, then?" Claus wanted to know.

"Back to economics. Back to the theory of rational expectations, which says that the government cannot rely on adjustments in monetary and fiscal policy to control unemployment and interest rates."

"That's monetarism," Wedik pointed out. He had learned that much about economics since he had been forced to do without Admiral Green.

"Yes, sir. In fact, the rational expectations school of thought, centered at the University of Minnesota, originated as an outgrowth of monetarism. Still, there's a difference, isn't there Professor Claus? Remember what you told me over the phone when I called you on Sunday morning?"

"Of course. I told you about rational expectations. It's a specialty of mine."

"You were urging your theory on Admiral Green."

"Naturally. It was the only proper thing to do when he asked me for my advice."

Mildred Wedik made a gesture of despair. "Will someone please explain rational expectations in simple terms?"

"I will," Clause volunteered. His gaze swept the room to include all in his explanation. "You see, most of the time people behave in a rational fashion in their private dealings. If they're in business, they try to maximize their profits, and if they're consumers, they try to maximize the satisfaction they get from goods and services."

"I wouldn't quarrel with that," the First Lady said. "But surely that doesn't mean everybody is always completely satisfied."

"No, of course not," Claus replied. "We're all constrained by the limitations of our circumstances."

"You mean, when I used to do the grocery shopping—before the Secret Service made me stop—I only had so much money to spend, and that was my limitation. That's pretty easy."

"I agree with you, Mrs. Wedik. But my point is that you were also rational in the sense that you used all the information you had at your disposal when you did the marketing."

"Of course, Professor Claus. I'm a careful shopper. Some people think that a President's wife doesn't need to count her pennies. But believe you me, Stanley and I have to watch our money just like everyone else."

"We understand, Mrs. Wedik," Alice said in a soothing tone.

"I get all the information available," the First Lady went on. "I compare the prices and quality of everything I buy."

"Especially big-ticket items like appliances or television sets?" Alice queried helpfully.

"Yes. It's really worthwhile doing comparison shopping for major purchases. I take time to do that very carefully."

"But you cannot know everything, can you?" Claus suggested.

"Of course not, but I use all the information I have, or at least all the information that's worth the time and trouble to get."

"So you economize on the use of information. You're limited by what you know, but you make careful use of all the available information."

"Correct, Professor. I know the prices of gifts are going to go up before Christmas, so I try to shop early."

"You don't always shop early, my dear," Wedik reminded his wife.

"Stanley, I do my best. If you would do some of the shopping yourself, you would know how much time it takes. Sometimes I do some last-minute Christmas shopping even though I know it will be more expensive. I admit it, Stanley. I just don't have time."

Alice interrupted this domestic dialogue to point out that Mrs. Wedik was certainly rational in her use of information.

172

She wasn't being fooled by the stores that were going to raise prices just before the holidays. Rather, knowing what was going to happen, she chose to pay the higher price because she couldn't take time away from other activities to shop when prices were lower.

"Stanley, you know all the social duties and responsibilities being First Lady puts on me," Mildred Wedik said with an aggrieved expression. "That's something I do for you. I should think you would appreciate what I do more than you do."

Wedik was sorry he had spoken up. "Of course, Mildred. You know I appreciate what you do for me—and for the country. You make the best use of your time and money with the information you have."

The First Lady was not quite mollified. "I am not fooled by the stores. I know what the prices are going to be."

"We all see that, Mrs. Wedik." Alice finally succeeded in defusing her indignation at her husband. "You have rational expectations about future prices, which means you use all the knowledge you have."

"Alice, I don't pretend to have perfect knowledge. Nobody can know what prices are going to be like. Sometimes things go up in price or down. I can't help that." Turning to her husband, "I do the best I can with the information I have."

Claus intervened. "That's what I mean when I talk about rational expectations. It's not part of the theory that everybody has exhaustive information, only that they do use all the information worth having. Which means that, by and large, in a competitive situation people are fooled mostly by events that are unpredictable. They have no pattern."

"If prices change by chance, then there's nothing I can do about it, is there Alice?" the First Lady persisted.

"No, Mrs. Wedik, there certainly isn't. You do take into account any systematic changes, those you can predict and act upon. What fool all of us shoppers from time to time are the unpredictable, random changes in the goods we buy."

"Yes, that's what I was trying to say, dear," said Wedik hurriedly. He wanted domestic tranquility.

Dannunzio had some difficulty containing his impatience with the fine points of communication between an old married couple. "What has this got to do with monetary policy, Professor Claus?"

"It's like this. If all those who spend money used all the information available, they also would use information about what the government policy is going to be—and what its effects are likely to be as well. If economists were consistent in their notion of equilibrium, say the balance of supply and demand, they ought to be talking about 'full equilibrium,' including the government as well as the private sector."

"So what has that got to do with Mrs. Wedik and her shopping?" Dannunzio grumbled.

"Everything!" Christopherson interposed violently. "You police are so blockheaded! Don't you see that if the typical consumer like Mrs. Wedik uses all the information available to predict market prices, she cannot be cheated or misled by any of the storekeepers."

"You mean she has to know everything that's going to happen in all the markets in which she trades?"

"No, no, Dannunzio! She may well be wrong, but if she uses all the available information, her guess about the future prices of things is as good as that of the sellers. They may all be wrong, but she cannot be manipulated or fooled because all the information is public and she can use it as well as any department store or grocer."

"I told Stanley that . . ." Mrs. Wedik began, but her protest was lost in the dialogue between the FBI agent and Christopherson, who was now beside himself. He threw all restraint to the winds. "If each economic actor uses all the information available to him, the government is as powerless to influence his actions as a storekeeper trying to manipulate a good shopper like Mrs. Wedik. If the government can't manipulate the purchases and production plans of individuals and businesses, then it can't control the real variables of the economy."

"You mean income and employment," Alice suggested.

"Right! Right!" Christopherson bit off the words. "The government can certainly influence the money supply and therefore the price level, but not real output or employment! The price level is only money!"

"You mean the rational expectations hypothesis still accepts the equation of exchange like other monetarists?" Alice was leading him on.

"Naturally. Inflation is everywhere a monetary phenomenon! We all accept that—all of us, whether we believe in the rational expectations hypothesis or not."

"But the point is?" Dannunzio asked. He was playing Alice's game of getting the Fed chairman to talk as much as possible.

Christopherson spoke emphatically. "The bottom line is that the rational expectations people agree with the monetarists that the government cannot manipulate the real economy. Its actions are foreseen insofar as they are systematic and not random. That means the consumers and businesspeople take appropriate action to discount them."

"In plain English," Claus explained, "if the government were to increase the money supply in order to increase demand and hence employment, firms would foresee that prices were going to rise, and they would not be fooled into increasing output and employment in the hopes of making a profit. They would see that their expenses for labor and materials would rise as much as the prices of the goods they sell, so that in real terms they would not be any better off. Prices would rise, but not the real aspects of the economy."

"Output and employment?" Dannunzio asked.

"Exactly."

"But don't output and employment change?" the FBI man asked.

"Sure, but these variations have to be the result of random forces that cannot be predicted. Most important, they cannot be the result of government policy. Random forces certainly can affect output and employment, according to the theory. In fact, the government can affect real elements of the economy only if it acts in a completely random, unpredictable fashion. Otherwise it would be systematic in its policies. The public would understand how the government is going to react, and would take measures to protect their individual interests, which would have the effect of neutralizing government policy."

Dannunzio was incredulous. "You mean that the only way government can be effective is if it does not have any rhyme or reason to its policies? If it does have a plan, it cannot carry its policies out without being frustrated by the reaction of those in the market?"

"The danger of an intrusion by the government," Claus responded, "is that it increases the uncertainty. But if the government is going to do something, as in changing the money supply, this should be announced in advance and done at one crack. This eliminates frustrating time lags in acquiring accurate information."

Christopherson was insistent again, lost in the passion of his chain of reasoning. "That's the message of Mrs. Wedik's marketing strategy. She's as smart as any government official. If prices are going to rise or fall, she won't be fooled into making contracts to buy or sell at today's prices, but will base her decisions on what the future is likely to bring."

"What do you make of the Keynesian policies of Dr. Sokolow, Mr. Christopherson?" Dannunzio fed the bait in tacit collusion with Alice Ritter.

"Doomed. They are doomed. Don't you see that they are based on fooling the public? All this talk of money illusion simply means that prices and wages tend to be sticky, so if the government increases the money supply or accelerates its own spending, people will be fooled into thinking real demand has gone up. Business will employ more people and produce more. Nonsense! All that is a snare and a delusion. All that will do is create more inflation. People are not fools. They will not fall for that line. Only nominal values will change. Prices will rise."

"And interest rates?" Alice queried.

"Interest rates will not decline in real terms. People make interest-bearing contracts based on the expected future rate of inflation. Nominal interest rates will rise with inflation, but the expected rate of inflation will be passed through and the real rate of interest, like all other real values, will be unaffected."

Robert Brittain threw up his hands. "Why all this economic theory when we're dealing with murder?"

"Because economic theory is leading us to the murderer of Marianne van Thuys," Alice informed him. "The murderer wanted Admiral Green to accept the theory of rational expectations. He got Marianne to defend it when the Admiral visited her. As we know, the plan succeeded. The admiral came down against the Keynesians."

Brittain was exasperated. "Stop talking in riddles! Who shot Marianne van Thuys?"

Alice looked at Claus. "We know, don't we, Professor? You were the one who coached Marianne in the theory of rational expectations, weren't you? It was too elaborate for a phone call. So you went to see her yourself. She was a pretty good pupil, wouldn't you say? I think you'd give her an A-plus in macroeconomics."

"Wait a minute!" Claus erupted. "You can't pin this on me! Yes, I talked economics with her, but that was all!"

"Alice, that's the second motive you were talking about," Dannunzio said. "A Keynesian shot Green, and a monetarist shot van Thuys. Sokolow and Claus! It all fits!"

"It doesn't fit," Alice contradicted him. "Professor Claus is telling the truth. All he did was coach Marianne.

"Professor Claus visited Marianne openly," Alice noted. "He knew he could have been spotted by some of the other residents of the apartment house. He would certainly be a prime suspect if he shot her. Then there's the fact that he was only a consultant to the Fed. He wasn't close enough to the government to know what was going on at the White House, or to feel that he had to save the country from the Keynesians."

Alice stopped and then continued slowly, "Professor Claus, when I said 'we know,' I'm sure you took my meaning, though you couldn't believe it. Do you believe it now?"

Bug-eyed, Claus turned toward Christopherson. "Martin?" he gasped.

The chairman of the Fed narrowed his eyes and clenched his teeth.

"Mr. Christopherson, you felt that you had to stop the Keynesians, didn't you?" Alice pressed him hard.

"Yes!" he shouted. "I had to stop them! Otherwise the Fed would have been dragooned into printing more and more money, desperately trying to control what cannot be controlled! Inflation would have run rampant over this country!"

"That was the reason for your conspiracy with Marianne van Thuys. When you learned she was Admiral Green's mistress, you got in touch with her and made her an offer she couldn't refuse. She was so successful with Admiral Green that you paid her increasingly large sums of money. I'd say Professor Claus was your paymaster."

"I delivered some envelopes to Marianne but I didn't know that they contained Christopherson's bribes," Claus answered. "I coached Marianne because Christopherson wanted me to, and because she was an influential woman in Washington. That was all."

"What was it about Marianne van Thuys that made her expendable?" Alice asked Christopherson. "There was, of course, the possibility of a national scandal. Suppose it became public knowledge that the chairman of the Fed had been manipulating national economic policies by paying a courtesan like Marianne to influence the man who would make the decision for the President. Wouldn't that be a pretty scandal! It might even have short-circuited those monetarist policies you so desperately wanted to put into effect. There might have been a rebellion against them in Congress."

"There might!" Christopherson snarled.

"You couldn't allow that to happen, could you? And it was all because of the disappearance of Admiral Green. His murder must have really shaken you because you had all your work to do over again. Only this time, Marianne van Thuys was of no use to you. She was a liability, knowing what she knew. There's another point. With Admiral Green's death, she could no longer sell her influence over him for money. There was only one way she could stay on your payroll. Blackmail."

Christopherson nearly strangled over his reply. "She wanted me to pay her forever!"

"So you silenced her forever. You promised to meet her by night in her apartment and pay the first installment for her secrecy. You didn't need keys. She willingly let you in. Only, instead of money you brought a gun. You were so nervous, you left the front door ajar. That was unlucky because Marianne certainly wouldn't have answered the bell when Frances called, and Frances wouldn't have been able to get in. But you were lucky you did the shooting before she got there. A minute later, and Frances Green would have seen you. While she was entering Marianne's apartment, you were scooting down the back stairs."

"Yes, Ritter, I did it!" Christopherson shouted. "Everything I ever did was in the public interest! That's why I shot Marianne van Thuys!"

"Sokolow and Christopherson, two of a kind," said Wedik somberly. "They just came to murder from opposite directions. Sokolow from the short run and Christopherson from the long run."

"In the long run they are both dead," said Alice Ritter.

20

The End

The *Chesapeake* came about at the command of John Ritter and headed back toward its Washington berth. Exhausted by the deadly game of cat and mouse, Alice Ritter paced the afterdeck accompanied by Sal Dannunzio. They were both young—and shared the same ambitious drive to advance in their organizations.

"You sure gave a demonstration of how to manipulate the mighty powers that be, Alice. How did you ever figure out what Green's position ultimately was on the Keynesian-monetarist debate?"

"Thanks for the compliment, Sal. Of course, I had the advantage of my talk with Professor Claus. Since he pushed rational expectations, and so did Marianne, it was a fair guess that he had been explaining it to her. She couldn't have been coached over the phone, and Christopherson, the only other possibility, wouldn't have taken the chance of visiting her himself. A consultant passing through the Fed would be a good choice."

"Too bad Green didn't simply tell you what he had decided."

"He was too much the professional navy officer for that. There was no 'need to know' on my part, and in the navy you don't confide top-level secrets except to those who need to know because they're part of the operation. However, when I met the admiral at the Pentagon on Sunday, he was fully decided about which course to take in his presentation to the cabinet. His agonizing decision was made. It crossed my mind that he had discovered a new line of reasoning that locked everything into place for him. And it occurred to me that it had come from Marianne van Thuys."

"Then you found what the new information was," Dannunzio guessed. "The rational expectations hypothesis. Chalk up one for you. Bob Brittain and I listened to the tape and missed the point completely."

"You couldn't see the point without the other clues, Sal. First of all, I knew that Green would jump at a hypothesis that short-circuited the long-run/short-run dilemma. Claus did that for him by claiming that that issue is largely irrelevant from the standpoint of public policy.

"The rational expectations people argue that government is simply impotent to manipulate the real variables—not just in the long run, as the traditional monetarists had argued, but never. Admiral Green was desperate for a way out, and rational expectations provided a way of ending his dilemma."

"Is that all you had to go on, Alice?" Dannunzio asked.

"No, there's a bit more. Lincoln helped me."

"I must say, that's an interesting thought. How did Honest Abe do that?"

Alice chuckled. "Consider what he said: 'You can fool all of the people some of the time, and some of the people all of the time, but you cannot fool all of the people all of the time.' What's that but rational expectations? The relevance struck me after I listened to the van Thuys tape. Not that Abe Lincoln ever heard of rational expectations as an economic theory!"

"Pretty good detective work, Alice. You should be with the FBI." The agent was frankly impressed by the chain of reasoning his friend had constructed.

"I'll stick with the navy, thank you, Sal. My daddy was a sailor. There's a song about that, but it's not quite ladylike."

From the rail, the pair watched the water churning as the *Chesapeake* moved ahead up the river.

"Alice, do you think that the rational expectations hypothesis is right?" Sal mused.

"I don't really know, Sal. It certainly is consistent with a lot of economic thinking about the behavior of individuals and markets. So it appeals to an orderly mind, like Admiral Green's. But there are those like Sokolow who don't believe in rationality in economic affairs to that extent, even in private transactions. And, of course, it's based on the equation of exchange and the questionable stability in the demand for money. So it comes from the monetarist camp, and I don't know whether that applies in anything but the long run, if then."

"Once you accept the idea of rationality, it is hard to resist the application of it to governmental actions as well as private ones. Brittain thinks everyone is rational in some sense . . . even the insane. I am glad I don't have to make up my mind about that one."

"So am I, Sal. But you know, I think that now President Wedik will go ahead and fight for a course to get the country out of the mess it's fallen into. The admiral taught him something about the nature of command."

"So did you, Alice."

The engines cut their speed as the harbor came into view.

"There's one thing about this case I still don't understand," Dannunzio said. "What was the point of all that talk about Geraldine Anderson if she's not guilty?"

"Well, I couldn't know for a fact that she was completely innocent. After all, we were dealing with circumstantial evidence, not mathematics. Suppose I had missed an essential clue. Suppose she had hired an assassin to kill Admiral Green. Suppose she was Sokolow's accomplice, or Christopherson's."

The FBI agent followed her train of thought. "You knew if you could trick Sokolow and Christopherson into confessing, that they alone were guilty, that would end the speculation about Anderson."

"I'm glad it worked out that way," Alice said. "I didn't ask President Wedik to invite her to join us on the *Chesapeake* because I didn't want to hurt Mrs. Green's feelings more than I had already. By the way, can you keep the Anderson-Green affair out of the news media?"

"I don't see why not. There's no need for us to interrogate Geraldine Anderson since we know she had no connection with the Green-van Thuys murders."

"I appreciate that," she told him. "I dreamed up this voyage to keep the discussion confidential. It was one way to make sure no reporters were hanging around. And I don't think there will be any leaks. No one aboard has any reason to reveal what we talked about."

The ship eased up to the dock. The passengers prepared to go ashore.

21
Epilogue

Three years later, the spanking-new guided missile destroyer *Harcourt Green* was ready to get underway. It was a beautiful day. Bright sun sparkled from the wavelets at the quay, almost blinding the crowd that had come to see her shove off. The cool breeze cut the warm Washington air.

The captain stood on the bridge. A uniformed arm was raised and the steam whistle screeched its three blasts to tell the world that a new ship was joining the fleet. At the command, bow and stern lines were cast off and the ship moved, gathering momentum, away from the dock.

The captain stood on the bridge and saw Salvatore Dannunzio standing on the dock. Their eyes met across the widening gap of water that separated them. Dannunzio blew the captain a kiss to the repeated triple-whooped blast of the destroyer. Alice Ritter waved back.

2,51